MW00872843

The Language of the Heart

An Introduction to Nichiren Daishonin's True Buddhism

Udumbara Foundation
Westport, Connecticut

Sanbō-in Temple
Fukuyama City, Japan

udumbarafoundation.org

6th Edition January 2023
Updated May 2023

Printed in USA

ISBN: 9798374330922
Imprint: Independently published

Back cover quote: "The Mongol Envoys," *Major Writings of Nichiren Daishonin*, (Nichiren Shoshu International Center, Tokyo, 1988), Vol. Five, p. 181.

Back cover calligraphy:
Sanbō-in (Temple of the Three Treasures)

DEDICATION

To all those who are seeking the truth,
And all those who are not.

I respect everyone deeply,
I do not despise anyone,
not even a little,
or look down on anyone with contempt,
because everyone has the capacity to
become a Buddha of
NamuMyōhōRengeKyō,
if they believe in
NamuMyōhōRengeKyō,
and practice.

Bodhisattva Jofukyō[1]

---

[1] Bodhisattva Jofukyō – Bodhisattva Never Despise. This passage is Reverend Raidō Hirota's paraphrase of a passage from Chapter 20 of the Lotus Sutra.

CONTENTS

PREFACE

The Truth is more rarely met with than . . . the udumbara flower[2] that blooms only once every three thousand years. . . .[3]

The format of our virtual meetings with our priest, Reverend Raidō Hirota, is Question and Answer and Discussion. Questions are submitted in advance to allow the priest time to consider each question, and to research, if necessary, so that his answers are not only substantive and thorough, but also align with both the Lotus Sutra and the writings of Nichiren Daishonin[4]. At a July 2022 meeting, a question was posed concerning the origin of NamuMyōhōRengeKyō[5]. The answer to that question can be found in "The True Buddha" section in this book. The answer corrects a falsehood taught by different Nichiren groups that I and so many other believers have wrongly

---

[2] Udumbara flower – a mythical flower in East Indian lore.

[3] "The Opening of the Eyes" Part II, *The Major Writings of Nichiren Daishonin*, Vol. Two, p. 163.

[4] Nichiren Daishonin - 1222-1282) the true Buddha who realized the Law of Namumyōhōrengekyō imbedded in the Lotus Sutra and established the Law as the means by which all livings beings can become enlightened.

[5] NamuMyōhōRengeKyō – the universal Law that is the heart of Nichiren Shoshu Buddhism and its reason for being.

believed for many years. Also updated is the description of *Renge*.

Reverend Hirota's answer, though perfectly logical, stunned all of us who were attending the meeting. Addressing our surprise and dismay for having been deceived, the priest responded by saying, "If you were taught something different that you now learn is wrong, reflect on why the teaching is wrong, and why the teaching was interpreted the way that it was. Seek the true meaning and direct your mind in the right direction. If you just switch to a new idea without reflecting on what was wrong with the old idea, the original idea will remain with you as an original trauma for your entire life. There is a saying in Japan that 'What you learn at the age of 3, stays with you for one hundred years or more.' So, what you should do is to not deny it. Face the mistakes and distortions you were taught and believed in, and change them into medicine to learn the correct interpretation."

It is due to the search for the Truth that I was compelled to edit this book. The basis of Buddhism is truth: The Truth about life itself. In these pages, I attempt to explain the basic principles of Nichiren Shoshu Buddhism[6]

---

[6] Nichiren Shoshu Buddhism – the religion that practices and studies the true teachings of Nichiren Daishonin.

to not only believers, but to anyone and everyone who knows nothing, or very little, about Buddhism. While the Buddhist practice is easy, Buddhist concepts are profound, broad, and difficult to explain and simplify. This modest book is an overview. It only skims the surface of Nichiren Shoshu Buddhism.

This 6th edition of *Language of the Heart* is, once again, a compilation of Nichiren Shoshu Shoshin-kai Shukyō Hōjin[7] priest Reverend Raidō Hirota's lectures and thoughts, with an addition of a few new essays; a few words of other Nichiren Shoshu Shoshin-kai Shukyō Hōjin priests; as well as thoughts and words of my own. I have organized and edited the various Buddhist concepts in a way that I hope make them more accessible and understandable to the non-believer as well as someone new to Buddhism. Even so, the concepts may be too rich. In my eagerness to convey this wonderful Buddhism to others, I may have provided too much information for newcomers. Read it slowly, in small doses. Let it find its way into your heart. My hope is that these teachings will touch your heart, as they have touched mine for many, many years, and inspire you to take the first

---

[7] Nichiren Shoshu Shoshin-kai Shukyō Hōjin, an independent, incorporated nonprofit organization of ordained Nichiren Shoshu priests, dedicated to protecting and teaching the True Teachings of Nichiren Daishonin.

steps towards your own enlightenment.

I cannot thank Kay Dubitsky, Karen Elders, Junko Miyoshi Meyerson, Junko Hokari and Asako Akai Ferguson enough for their translations. Without their painstaking effort, we would not have the wonderful teachings of Nichiren Daishonin's True Buddhism in English. To longtime believer, Michael Paris, I am deeply grateful for your keen eye and thoroughness, as well as your eagerness to help. Your suggestions have made this a better book. I also express deep gratitude for those people whose questions about life and Buddhism generated the answers that are the substance of this book. And for those people who had asked me to recommend a book on Buddhism, thank you, for you inspired me to sit down and write this book. Finally, and above all, I thank Reverend Hirota for his support, his encouragement, his tireless endeavor as a teacher of the True Law, and for his example as an ordinary, real-life person who is a true seeker of the Way.

Peach Pair
Author / Editor
January 2023

THE

LANGUAGE

OF THE

HEART

I

Fundamentals

What is Buddhism?

What is a Buddha?

What is the Buddha's Dharma?

The Purpose of Religion

What is religion?

A religion is something that one relies on to define life and to guide one in life.

The purpose of a religion should be to provide a system of beliefs that eliminates delusion, awakens all people to the true reality of life, and saves all living things. A true religion is one that does not discriminate against anyone, and leads all living things—whether human, plant or animal; whether feeling or non-feeling; whether good or evil—to achieve the highest state of awareness. And a true teaching is one that affects everyone the same, whether one believes it or not.

Buddhism in General and Specific

Buddhism is a system of beliefs based on the teachings of a Buddha—an enlightened One. The difference between Buddhism and other major religions of the world, including Christianity, Islam, Judaism and Hindu, is that Buddhism is Law-centric and not God-centric. The religions of Christianity, Islam, Hindu and Judaism believe that God has existed forever, and is the creator of everything. These beliefs differ greatly from Buddhism.

In general, Buddhism teaches that no one created life. That said, there are many different Buddhist sects, and many different Buddhist beliefs. The specific Buddhism under discussion in this text is Nichiren Shoshu. The fundamental belief of the religion of Nichiren Shoshu Buddhism is that there is one ultimate Law governing all things. This Law has always existed; the Buddha did not create it. The Buddha is a person – a human being just like you and me – who realized that such a Law existed. Thus, in Buddhism the Law existed first, and has existed since the infinite past – the Buddha came later.

Another important belief in Buddhism is that there is a reason for everything. To explain this briefly, the emergence—or the coming into existence—of all things, such as human life, animals, plant life, even stars, planets, sky, water, and so on, is a result of a complex series of causes and conditions that occur in time and space. Thus, it can be said that Buddhism is the study of life.

The Law

Dharma is a Sanskrit word, which means *Hō* in Japanese and "Law" in English. The *Dharma* or Law is the Buddha's ultimate truth. What is the ultimate truth? It is NamuMyōhōRengeKyō[8], the ultimate Law of life and death throughout the universe. It is called the *Mystic Law*, and it is the center of belief in Nichiren Shoshu Buddhism.

MyōhōRengeKyō or NamuMyōhōRengeKyō is the *Mystic Law*. What does this phrase mean?

Namu means devotion with one's whole mind and one's whole life. This devotion is to *MyōhōRengeKyō*.

Myō is the mystery and wonder of the life of all people and all things. This concept of *myō* means that even selfish, egotistical people, such as ourselves, who are common mortals, also have Buddha-nature and therefore can realize enlightenment. *Myō* also indicates that everything, even insects, plants and dead wood have a soul.

Hō refers to the Law. This Law constitutes all living things on this earth as well as all things throughout the entire universe. To teach the mystery of life is to teach about the Law.

---

[8] Pronounced- Nan~meo – ho – ren – gay – key-o.

Renge is the lotus flower. The lotus can be a very large plant, producing leaves as large as 2 to 3 feet or more, and its flowers can grow nearly as big. The lotus plant has a distinctive conical yellow seed pod at the center of its blossom, which is the female reproductive structure. Encircling the seed pod are rows of stamen which are the male reproductive organs. Once pollinated, the seeds become evident in the mature flower before the petals fall off. Because the blossom, which is the effect, and the seeds which are the cause, exist at the same time, this makes the plant a complete entity. Thus this exquisitely beautiful and impressive flower is a perfect example of flowering plants that contain both flower and seeds at the same time. That is probably why Shakyamuni chose the lotus flower, the national flower of India, as the metaphor to illustrate the wonderful aspect of *Myōhō,* the Mystic Law, which is that cause and effect are present simultaneously. Therefore, *Renge* indicates that the Law of *MyōhōRengeKyō* is both the cause of enlightenment (Buddhahood), and the effect - enlightenment (Buddhahood) itself. Everything exists in one entity. To put it another way, one entity contains everything. The entity of human life and all life is *MyōhōRengeKyō.* And "cause and effect" is absolute, and continues on forever.

Kyō means teaching or sutra. It refers to the Buddha's teaching. It is the Buddha's preaching of the Law. *Kyō* indicates the "pure and far-reaching voice" of the Buddha. The truth.

NamuMyōhōRengeKyō is the expression of life's dynamic continuum in one phrase. NamuMyōhōRengeKyō is actually life condensed. It can be compared to concentrated orange juice; it is *life concentrate*. NamuMyōhōRengeKyō is our life.

The concepts and teachings inherent in the Law of NamuMyōhōRengeKyō are set forth in the scripture known as the Lotus Sutra. The Lotus Sutra was one of Shakyamuni Buddha's last teachings. NamuMyōhōRengeKyō is the only religion that teaches about life – what life is. It teaches that life itself is the Law; that the Law is within us, and that the Law is inherent in every living thing. It also teaches that the seed of Buddhahood is the fruit of Buddhahood. NamuMyōhōRengeKyō is both the seed and the fruit of Buddhahood. It is both cause and effect.

The Law is above and beyond any god. It is an intangible that cannot be grasped or seen. It is incomparable; there is no other Law like it. There is only NamuMyōhōRengeKyō. NamuMyōhōRengeKyō, the *Mystic Law* of cause and effect, works the same in everyone's life whether one believes it or not.

Buddha

When the Law and the person merge, and the person embodies the Law—incorporates the Law into his or her life, and his or her behavior demonstrates that he or she is living with full awareness of the Law—this is Buddha. One who understands the Law of *MyōhōRengeKyō* is a Buddha. Such a person is awakened to the true reality of existence and the ultimate truth of life, and helps others achieve the same realization. A Buddha teaches everyone without discrimination.

Buddha-nature

Christians believe that man is basically evil, and can only be saved if Jesus enters into one's heart. Buddhism believes that man is basically good because all people have Buddha-nature at the core of their lives.

Yes, you have Buddha-nature within you. Would you believe that a rug has Buddha-nature? Trees have Buddha-nature, so do flowers and grass. Even the gravel in a driveway and the asphalt on a road have Buddha-nature. The birds and bees have Buddha-nature, as do rats and vermin. The air and water have Buddha-nature too. As you've probably surmised, everything has Buddha-nature, even the dead.

What is Buddha-nature? NamuMyōhōRengeKyō is Buddha-nature. Buddha-nature is the life of Buddha. It is the seed of Buddhahood contained within all life. It is what gives all life the potential to realize Buddhahood or become enlightened. Since everything has the seed of Buddhahood, anyone and anything can become enlightened.

There are not different kinds of Buddha-natures; there is only one Buddha-nature. The Buddha-nature is the same in all things.

II

The Lineage of Buddhism

It is generally believed that there is only one Buddha—Shakyamuni Gautama Buddha from India who lived nearly three thousand years ago. That, however, is not true. Over the course of eternity throughout the universe there have been an uncountable number of Buddhas. Out of all those Buddhas, only two will be discussed here: Shakyamuni and Nichiren Daishonin.

The Life of Shakyamuni

During the prehistoric ages of this world—before written records were kept and human life was primitive—six ancient Buddhas made their advent to teach and guide people. The world's religions developed from these early Buddhist teachings. The historical Buddha, Shakyamuni of India, was the seventh ancient Buddha on this planet. He was the first Buddha of recorded time. And it is his teachings that are the basis of all Buddhisms today.

Shakyamuni literally means sage of the Shakya tribe. There is much dispute as to when Shakyamuni was born. Some say he lived about twenty-five hundred years ago, while the traditions of China and Japan record Shakyamuni's birth as being on the 8th day of the fourth month in the year 1029 B.C.E. in what is today, Nepal, and passing away in the middle of the night on the 15th day of the second month in the year 949 B.C.E. He was born as Prince Siddhartha Gautama, son of King Shuddhodana of the Shakya tribe.

As a young prince, Siddhartha was surrounded by luxury and grandeur, and was protected from witnessing the misfortunes of others. Despite the care the palace took to protect him, Siddhartha, as a young man, became aware of the poverty beyond the royal gates. The misery he witnessed was so troubling that it aroused in him an intense desire to understand the cause of human suffering, and the causes of the four sorrows of birth, old age, sickness and death. While still a young man, he renounced the secular world—which meant leaving his wife, the beautiful Princess Yasodhara, and child, Rahula, and giving up all rights to his inheritance—to pursue religious life.

He first studied Hinduism and yogic meditation with the Brahmins. Not finding the answers to the troubling dilemma of the human condition, Siddhartha left the Brahmins after a few years to pursue severe ascetic practices such as fasting and self-mortification. He undertook these assiduous practices more vigorously and rigorously than anyone, because his pursuit of the true meaning of life was more earnest than others. But when he realized these practices did not lead to the awakening he so desired, he rejected all of them. He then went and sat under a papal tree (now referred to as the Bodhi tree) where he entered into deep meditation, and in a matter of days realized enlightenment. At that time, he would have been between the ages of 29 and 35.

After he had attained enlightenment, Shakyamuni wanted to pass on to everyone what he himself had realized. The status of the persons he instructed did not matter to him. Whether it was a man or a woman, a king or a pauper, a doctor or a leper, he taught everyone equally. He taught so many teachings over the course of his lifetime to everyone he met, that it is said he taught altogether some eighty thousand teachings. The most significant of his teachings was the Lotus Sutra (Sanskrit: *Saddharma Pundarika Sutra)* which he taught in the last eight years of his life. The Lotus Sutra was the crown jewel of his lifetime achievements.

For the ninety days following Shakyamuni's death, from the 8th day of the fourth month to the 15th day of the seventh month, one thousand of the Buddha's most learned disciples were brought together to discuss and compile all the sutras he had taught over the fifty years of his preaching life. This gathering of scholars and wise men was called the Chamber of the First Council. The Council was organized by Ajatashatru, King of Magadha. That the Council was held in Magadha was not so unusual since it was on Eagle Peak in the Kingdom of Magadha that Shakyamuni Buddha preached the Lotus Sutra. But what is truly extraordinary and miraculous is that it was King Ajatashatru who organized and sponsored it. Ajatashatru had spent the early half of his life as one of Shakyamuni's most vehement adversaries. He obstructed the progress of Buddhism every chance he could. He plotted against the Buddha and caused injury and even death to some of Shakyamuni's disciples. Not until just prior to the time Shakyamuni began teaching the Lotus Sutra did King Ajatashatru begin to come around and have a change of heart. Still, it took another eight years for him to completely relinquish his evil ways, repent of his sins and surrender his heart to Buddhism. That transformation took place on the 15th day of the second month in the year 949 B.C.E., the last day of Shakyamuni Buddha's life. Therefore, it is due to the transformation of this one-time foe of the Buddha that we have the Lotus Sutra today.

The Four Noble Truths

Many people who are not familiar with Buddhism have heard of the four noble truths. The concept of the four noble truths and the eightfold path was taught by Shakyamuni not long after his enlightenment. These concepts are a part of the Hinayana[9] sutras.

---

[9] Hinayana – Theravada Buddhism (Lesser Vehicle) primarily concerned with self-salvation and elimination of desires.

The four noble truths are: 1) all existence is suffering; 2) suffering is caused by desire; 3) eliminating desire eradicates suffering and brings about emancipation; 4) eradication of desire can be achieved by the eightfold path. The eightfold path is: right views, right thinking, right speech, right action, right way of life, right endeavor, right mindfulness and right meditation.

In the first three weeks after his enlightenment, Shakyamuni taught *The Flower Garland Sutra*[10]. In this sutra, he spoke about the mysteries of life: the interrelatedness of all things. These teachings were so esoteric no one could understand them. Since Shakyamuni at first taught the *Flower Garland Sutra*—teachings that were obscure and unfathomable—it was as if his audience was blind and deaf. They could neither see nor hear the teachings. His words meant nothing to them. Yet, because the teachings were so impressive and scholarly, they were like a sparkling object, an extraordinary wonder that captured people's attention, and gave people a sense of the greatness of Buddhism. Once Shakyamuni had attracted an audience, he began by teaching at the lowest level, which reflected the state of existence of the people, who were nearly barbaric, living during that ancient time. These were the Hinayana

---

[10] The Flower Garland Sutra – (Skt) *Avatamasaka* Sutra. (Jp) *Kegon* Sutra.

teachings, such as the four noble truths and the eightfold path. With these teachings, he began to slowly cultivate the people's minds so that they could gradually understand deeper concepts.

The Hinayana sutras were similar to thoughts, philosophies and ideas the people already knew, and could therefore easily understand. In these sutras, Shakyamuni laid out very specific and direct causes and effects and punishments: If you did this, such and such would happen. If you did that, you would have such and such effect. Shakyamuni taught the people as though they were children, telling them to have right thinking, right actions, etc. Just as parents teach their children right and wrong, he told the people not to cheat, not to steal, not to lie, not to do bad things. This was something anyone could understand, even those who did not have knowledge or deep comprehension. During the Hinayana period, people thought that Buddhism was nothing more than moral ideals. But not everyone could be saved by these teachings. Gradually, in time, and as the people's capacity to understand increased, Shakyamuni moved on to higher teachings. The Buddha was determined to save everyone, even those who committed crimes. The earlier teachings did not grant this. They could not offer salvation to all – not to the learned, to women, to evil people, to insentient beings. The Lotus Sutra is the only teaching in which Shakyamuni promised that everyone could be saved. It took Shakyamuni more than forty years to prepare the people of his time for the teachings that would save all mankind. It was not until the last eight years of his life that he finally taught the Lotus Sutra.

Particularly in the Western world, people tend to think that there is only one Buddhism. But because the Buddha taught differently depending on the audience, on the circumstances of the people he was addressing, and on the time period in which he was teaching, there are various teachings and various levels of teachings. For example, Zen Buddhism, which relies on wordless transmission of concepts from mind to mind and not on doctrinal study, is completely different from the Lotus Sutra. The Lotus Sutra was taught at the end of the Buddha's life. It was only at the end of his life that Shakyamuni was able to teach the teaching that he had in truth wanted to teach at the very beginning. In the Lotus Sutra, he explains his own enlightenment, and the way for all living beings to realize enlightenment. So to be clear, the four noble truths, the eightfold path, and meditation on the "void" do not lead to enlightenment. Such teachings were early teachings of

Shakyamuni's intent was to cultivate, discipline, inspire awe, and prepare people for the highest teachings.

Lotus Sutra

All of Shakyamuni's teachings over the course of his entire lifetime are united in the Lotus Sutra. The Lotus Sutra is the reason for his advent in this world. In chapter 2 of this august work Shakyamuni announced, "After the Buddha's [preparatory] teaching he must [now] proclaim the perfect truth."[11] In the 11th chapter the Buddha declared, "Since I attained the enlightenment of the Buddha, I have expounded many sutras in innumerable worlds. This sutra is the most excellent. To keep this sutra is to keep me."[12] And in chapter 23 he proclaimed, "Just as the sea is larger than the rivers, this *Sutra of the Lotus Flower of the Wonderful Law* is more profound than any of the other sutras expounded by Buddhas. . . . Just as the Buddha is the king of the Law, this sutra is the king of all sutras. . . . This sutra

---

[11] *The Threefold Lotus Sutra*, Translated by Bunnō Katō et al. (Weatherhill/Kosei, New York/Tokyo,1975), p. 55
[12] *The Lotus Sutra*, Translated by Senchu Murano, (Nichiren Shu Headquarters, Tokyo, 1974), pp. 175-176

saves all living beings."[13]

Among the principles illuminated in the Lotus Sutra are:

- The true reality of all existence is that all life contains the life of Buddha, therefore all life is equal.
- The one great reason for all Buddhas to appear in the world is to open the wisdom of the Buddha for all living things, to show the Buddha wisdom to all living things, to cause all living beings to be enlightened, and to encourage all living beings to enter the path of Buddha wisdom.
- All people regardless of gender or status or condition of life, can realize Buddhahood through faith in the Lotus Sutra.
- The existence of Buddha is eternal, the Buddhist Laws of truth are never-ending, and all people, as well as all things, possess eternal life.

The Lotus Sutra also predicts that a votary would come along during the 500-year period following the second millennium after the death of Shakyamuni and reveal the true teachings of the Lotus Sutra.

---

[13] Idem, pp. 277

The True Buddha

The True Buddha – the Buddha who taught the true cause of enlightenment – made his appearance about 2200 years after Shakyamuni Buddha's passing. He was born in a fishing village in Chiba Prefecture on the east coast of Japan on the 16th day of the second month in the year 1222, and was named Zennichimaro. (Later he would be known as Nichiren Daishonin.) Unlike Shakyamuni Buddha who was born a prince in a royal family, Zennichimaro was born of poor lineage, and openly spoke of it. "In this life," he wrote, "I was born in poverty of humble parentage; I grew up in the house of a *candala*." In the Indian caste system, the *candala* is the lowest class. This class consists of fishermen, jailers, slaughterers and followers of other "unclean" trades. Yet, despite having been born into such lowly circumstances, Zennichimaro's parents saw to it that he was granted an education.

Between the ages of 12 and 16, Zennichimaro attended Seichō-ji, a temple seminary on Mount Kiyosumi, near his home. Initially, he studied the fundamentals of Buddhism, and received a general education. Zennichimaro was exceptionally mature and precocious for his age, for as early as age 12 he began to pray for wisdom. He was also troubled by the magnitude of the peoples' suffering, and wanted to understand what caused people to suffer, and how it could be eliminated. Remarkably, in those early years, he had a great realization in perceiving truths about the essence of life. But that was not enough. He knew that he would need to support his realizations with theory and documentary proof; and that that would require extensive study.

At age 16, Zennichimaro shaved his head and took his vows as a priest. At his ordination, he was given the name Zeshō-bō Renchō, which for him held a profound meaning. (*Zeshō* indicates sacred person under the sun; *Renchō* means lotus growth or sprouting from a lotus).

Soon after ordination, Zeshō-bō Renchō departed Mount Kiyosumi in pursuit of the knowledge that would support his earlier realizations. For the next 16 years or so, he traveled to Kamakura, Kyoto and Nara, Japan's three great learning centers of the 13th-century. At these centers, Zeshō-bō Renchō endeavored to study and practice the Great Vehicle, Mahayana Buddhism, which was practiced in the countries of northeast Asia, namely India, China, Korea and Japan. In searching for the teaching that defined and proclaimed the supreme Law that he had realized in his youth, he also studied the doctrines of Hinayana Buddhism, other major Buddhist sects, as well as Confucianism.

Renchō was structured and systematic in his studies. Without prejudice, he engaged in the practice of each sect and group to understand the substance of their original doctrine as well as their underlying principle or law. He carefully documented his progress and his realizations concerning the teachings of the various sects and their relative merit. What he was searching for was the teaching that unequivocally affirmed that every life, whether human or non-human, sentient or insentient, was equal, and that each individual life possessed the Buddha-life or Buddha-nature. One by one, he experienced and compared the teachings. And in the end, he had to reject all of the major Buddhist sects of the day, including Shingon, Zen, Jōdo and Ritsu. He found the doctrines of these sects, and the scriptures they followed, to be incomplete, borrowed, limited, or completely wrong. Having studied all the Buddhist texts, and experienced firsthand their practices, he became convinced that the true doctrine of Shakyamuni Buddha was only contained in the Lotus Sutra, and that all teachings of Buddhism could be found united within the one scripture of the Lotus Sutra. Thus, he embraced the Lotus Sutra exclusively, and championed it as the only teaching containing the truth that he had perceived in his youth.

Renchō determined that the Lotus Sutra offered complete salvation and absolute mercy, since its doctrine teaches that all living things may be granted a way of life the same as that of Buddha. He also perceived that the essence of the sutra was contained in its title.

Saddharma-pundarika-sutra is the Sanskrit title of the Lotus Sutra. It was translated into Chinese as 妙法蓮華経 (*Miao-fa-lien-hua-ching*) in 406 C.E. by Kumarajiva[14]. There are several extant Chinese translations of the Lotus Sutra. But because of its elegance and excellence, Kumarajiva's was the translation Zeshō-bō Renchō, as well as most religious scholars in China and Japan preferred.[15]

As many may know, formal Japanese uses Chinese characters as its alphabet. In Japanese, this alphabet is called *kanji*. The Japanese pronunciation of the *kanji* characters

---

[14] Kumarajiva – (344-413) an Indian Buddhist monk and scholar who, as a child, traveled with his mother around India and other nations to study Buddhism. Because of his renown as a Mahayana scholar fluent in Chinese he was evidentially given the position of Teacher of the Nation in the Chinese capital of Ch'ang-an where he committed himself to translating Buddhist scriptures, including the Lotus Sutra, into Chinese.

[15] *The Threefold Lotus Sutra*, Bunnō Katō, et als, Weatherhill/Kosei, 1975

妙法蓮華経 is *MyōhōRengeKyō*[16]. Thus, the Japanese title of the Lotus Sutra is *MyōhōRengeKyō*. Renchō came to realize that the title, *MyōhōRengeKyō* was the essential part of the Lotus Sutra, for *MyōhōRengeKyō* is the Mystic Law itself.

There is no phrase within the Lotus Sutra that includes *Namu*. *Namu* in essence means "return your life to *Myōhō*," or believe in *MyōhōRengeKyō* with your whole life, as though it is your life itself. This is the central teaching of the Lotus Sutra. The entire Lotus Sutra is concentrated in its title: *MyōhōRengeKyō*. By adding *Namu* to *MyōhōRengeKyō* implies "I believe in, or I devote myself to the truth of the Mystic Law."

NamuMyōhōRengeKyō was not created or discovered by Nichiren Daishonin. As the Lotus Sutra was brought to Japan as early as the 6th or 7th century C.E. (or perhaps before) upon the request of Prince Shōtoku, the 2nd son of the 31st Emperor or Japan[17], there were people who had studied the Lotus Sutra before Nichiren, who was born in the 13th century. In the various temples where he had studied from childhood as an acolyte and during the sixteen

---

[16] MyōhōRengeKyō – the English translation is the *Teaching of the Mystic Law of Cause and Effect.*
[17] "Letter to Myomitsu Shonin," *The Major Writings of Nichiren Daishonin,* Vol. Five, pg. 191.

years studying in the major religious centers of Japan, priests and parishioners studied and recited the Lotus Sutra along with other sutras and other Buddhas. They chanted both *Namuamidabutsu*[18] and *NamuMyōhōRengeKyō* together. They combined these practices with practicing many other cultural rituals of the time. Based on all he had learned through his rigorous studies Nichiren Daishonin, chose to center his faith only on chanting NamuMyōhōRengeKyō, and was the first to have faith in, and practice the Lotus Sutra exclusively without any additional practices or beliefs.

At age 32, after sixteen long years of intense study, and armed with the absolute certainty of the Lotus Sutra's veracity, Renchō returned to Seichō-ji temple, where he had been ordained, to officially announce his findings. The day before his public announcement he requested to change his name. This was required because his name, Zeshō-bō Renchō, was bestowed on him by his teacher Dozenbo at the time of his ordination. Then, to prepare for his presentation, he secluded himself within the temple grounds. No one, not his colleagues, teachers, or family, had any idea of what was about to come; which at that time would have been a

---

[18] Namuamidabutsu – Devotion to Amida Buddha.

reckoning that would turn Buddhism on its head.

At noon on the 28th day of the fourth month in the year 1253, Zeshō-bō Renchō left his sanctum and went to the public square at Seichō-ji temple where an audience of his peers and local folk had eagerly gathered to hear his first sermon on what he had learned during his 16 years of travel and dedicated study. As he stood before his audience, it can be imagined that he pressed his palms together reverently and voiced with full resolve, "*NamuMyōhōRengeKyō* is the supreme Law, and the true and absolute practice of Buddhism for this age." He then announced that as of that day NamuMyōhōRengeKyō would be the sole practice that he would devote his life to.

In later years, Nichiren Daishonin would explain the significance of this phrase in his writing, "The One Essential Phrase":

...The Lotus Sutra defines our life as the Buddha's life, our mind as the Buddha's wisdom and our actions as the Buddha's behavior....NamuMyōhōRengeKyō is only one phrase but it contains the essence of the entire sutra....Everything has its essential point, and the heart of the Lotus Sutra is its title, NamuMyōhōRengeKyō. Truly, if you chant this in the morning and evening, you are correctly reading the entire Lotus Sutra.... A Law this easy to embrace and this easy to practice was taught

for the sake of all mankind in this evil age of the Latter Day of the Law.[19]

After proclaiming the supremacy of the Law of the Lotus Sutra, and his commitment to it, Renchō lectured on his findings and realizations, and exposed, in detail, the errors in the teachings of the major Buddhist sects. When he concluded his sermon, he announced that he was changing his name to "Nichiren." (Nichiren means sun-lotus. The sun illuminates all. The lotus flower, having both flower and seed at the same time, indicates the simultaneity of cause and effect.) The significance of this name suggests Nichiren attained enlightenment by himself.

His sermon inflamed negative passions. Most of the audience were up in arms. It was radical. How could someone, who was no more than an itinerant priest at best, disparage their beliefs, disregard tradition, and advocate belief in ideas that seemed foreign, radical and fanatical? It was offensive. At once, chaos ensued at what was expected to be a tranquil and celebratory occasion.

The local lord of the district, Tojō Kagenobu, was roiling with anger. As a devout believer of one of the

---

[19] *The Major Writings of Nichiren Daishonin,* (Nichiren Shoshu International Center, Tokyo, 1979), Vol. One, pp. 221-222.

Buddhist sects refuted by Nichiren, Kagenobu decided Nichiren was a dangerous threat that had to be silenced. He summoned his samurai straightaway and they together plotted his demise.

Dozenbō, Nichiren's former teacher, was a senior priest at Seichōji. He was also an ardent believer in one of the Buddhist sects Nichiren had invalidated in his lecture. Lord Kagenobu was also his patron. Feeling the anger mounting against his former student, and as a cleric of one of the other sects, Dozenbō could have readily joined the angry crowd in plotting against Nichiren.

But Nichiren had been one of Dozenbo's favorite acolytes, with such bright prospects. Growing uneasy with the mounting rage, Dozenbo took pity on Nichiren. As an act of mercy, Dozenbo summoned two junior priests, and hastily organized a plan of escape. The two junior priests rushed into action, ushering Nichiren away from the mayhem, and escorting him through a secret passage that led into the woods where he was allowed to escape freely.

Twilight set in as Nichiren ran for his life along a foot path in the forest. It was an ironic ending to a day, that only a few hours earlier had begun with Nichiren proclaiming, in broad daylight, the true Buddhism for the modern age that would save all mankind.

Thus began Nichiren Daishonin's turbulent life as the votary of the Lotus Sutra. The circumstances and events of his life fulfilled the prophecies of the Lotus Sutra. Twenty-two years later, following two exiles, a foiled execution, and numerous attempts on his life, the Daishonin would write:

It would be easier to walk naked in a raging fire, easier to take up Mt. Sumeru in one's hands and toss it away, easier to hoist a great stone on one's back and walk across the ocean than to do what I have done. To establish the True Law in this country of Japan is indeed a difficult thing.[20]

Nichiren Daishonin passed away peacefully at the age of 61 on the 13th day of the 10th month in the year 1282. During his lifetime, he revealed the direct path to enlightenment that has, since the infinite past, lead all Buddhas to enlightenment; and he provided the true teachings, the true object of worship, and a concise practice to achieve that enlightenment. None of this was accomplished by Shakyamuni Buddha. On the day that Shakyamuni died, he issued a warning: "Follow the Law,

---

[20] On the Selection of the Time," *The Major Writings of Nichiren Daishonin*, (Nichiren Shoshu International Center, Tokyo, 1985) Vol. Three. p. 184.

not the person." However, Shakyamuni himself did not identify the Law which he had realized and had been enlightened by. Instead, he described it, praised it and alluded to it in the Lotus Sutra. His life's purpose was to teach the Lotus Sutra. Nichiren Daishonin's life's purpose was to unlock the secrets in the depths of the Lotus Sutra, identify and establish the universal Law, to reveal that all life is equal, and provide a simple and direct means for all living things to realize enlightenment. Shakyamuni was the true Buddha for his age. Nichiren Daishonin is the True Buddha for this age. Even so, the warning that Shakyamuni Buddha issued on his deathbed, to "Follow the Law, not the person," remains the guiding principle in Nichiren Daishonin's Buddhism. It is through the Law that one becomes enlightened. Because the person practices the Law, the person is worthy of respect. Thus, the Law is supreme, not the Buddha. The Law is worshipped, not the person.

III

Nichiren Shoshu

Nichiren Shoshu means Nichiren's true teachings, or the true teachings of Nichiren. Nichiren Shoshu is a Japanese Buddhism. It is a religion dedicated to teaching the Buddhism of Nichiren Daishonin.

Nichiren Shoshu Buddhism believes in the absolute equality of all life—that all things possess Buddha-nature. The objective of this Buddhism is the enlightenment of all living things.

The Teachings of Nichiren Shoshu

The basic teachings of Nichiren Shoshu are represented in the doctrine of the Three Great Secret Laws. The Three Great Secret Laws are the only precepts of the religion. They are: 1) the object of worship of the Eternal Buddha; 2) the sanctuary of the Eternal Buddha and; 3) the invocation of the Eternal Buddha.

The object of worship is the Gohonzon. *Honzon* is a Japanese word that means object of respect, and *Go* is an honorific title. The Gohonzon is a mandala that allows one to view one's mind and see all the various states of being within, including the condition of Buddha. The Gohonzon is a physical representation of the Law.

The sanctuary is the place where the Gohonzon is enshrined. It is an area removed from evil.

The invocation is NamuMyōhōRengeKyō intoned by believers.

It is the study and practice of these three basic ideals which form the essence of the Buddhism of Nichiren Shoshu.

To explain these a little further, the Gohonzon of the

Eternal Buddha represents the soul of Buddha. According to the teachings of Buddhism, it is by chanting NamuMyōhōRengeKyō to Gohonzon in the sanctuary—the place where Gohonzon is enshrined—that one can open the wisdom of Buddha and perceive eternal life. Through this simple practice, one can experience an inner peace and tranquility in daily life.

However, the invocation of NamuMyōhōRengeKyō in Nichiren Shoshu, is a form of chanting which is performed not only for oneself, it is also for leading others to enlightenment. NamuMyōhōRengeKyō must be chanted for others, for society and for the sake of righteousness. It is only by believing in the Three Great Secret Laws and study and practice, that one can gain the same heart as the true Buddha, Nichiren Daishonin.

The Practice

The practice of Nichiren Shoshu is the recitation of the title and two chapters (2nd and 16th) of the Lotus Sutra. The basis for this can be found in Nichiren Daishonin's writings. He wrote, "Among the entire twenty-eight chapters, the *Hoben* [2nd] and *Juryo* [16th] chapters are particularly outstanding. The remaining are all in a sense the branches and leaves of these two chapters. Therefore, I recommend that you practice reading the prose sections of the *Hoben* and *Juryo* chapters."[21]

To recite these two chapters from the Lotus Sutra in the morning and evening is considered the secondary practice. To chant and protect the title of the Lotus Sutra, NamuMyōhōRengeKyō, is the essential and primary practice.

The reason for having faith and practicing this Buddhism is to realize that the Buddha's life is within your life and all life. True value in life comes from seeking enlightenment. The purpose of life is to realize the Buddha-nature within, and to make NamuMyōhōRengeKyō the basis of every life activity. Striving to have NamuMyōhōRengeKyō in your heart and mind, and trying to achieve a life that is appropriate for the condition of Buddha that is within each human being is the true Way of the practitioners of Nichiren Shoshu Buddhism.

---

[21] "The Recitation of the Hoben and Juryo Chapters of the Lotus Sutra." *The Major Writings of Nichiren Daishonin* (Nichiren Shoshu International Center, Tokyo, 1990), *Vol. Six, p.10,*

Why We Chant Rather than Meditate

1. In meditation, only the individual who meditates benefits. This Buddhism is not only for the individual's enlightenment, it is for the enlightenment of all mankind and all other life forms. The only way non-human forms of life can become enlightened is by being exposed to the chanting of NamuMyōhōRengeKyō – hearing it, or by osmosis. When human beings chant, they sow the seed of Buddhahood in all the various objects in their environment.

2. One chants so that other human beings can hear it and thus receive the seed of Buddhahood.

3. The Buddha-nature in all life throughout the universe is summoned when one chants.

4. Chanting is unifying. One can chant with people of any nation because they are chanting in the Buddha's language and not in the language of any one country. When two or more people chant together there is harmony at that moment—world peace is achieved in the moment in that environment.

5. In meditation, one closes one's eyes and tries to control one's thoughts in an effort to separate

oneself from the outside world. By contrast, in true Buddhism all the senses are engaged in the practice, because enlightenment exists in all conditions of life.

a. **Seeing.** The eyes are open to see the Gohonzon (which represents Buddha) and the altar ("sanctuary"). This is also an expression of seeing clearly.

b. **Hearing.** The ears hear the chanting, which is enlightenment itself, and the ringing of the bell is the music offered to the Buddha

c. **Smelling.** The nose smells the fragrant incense which is offered to purify the environment for the Buddha

d. **Tasting.** Fruit is placed on the altar as an offering of food to the Buddha

e. **Touching.** The prayer beads, held in our hands, represent the body of the Buddha and the body of human beings. This signifies that Buddha exists within our human bodies.

f. **Thinking.** From our scattered thoughts arise the pure mind of Buddhahood.

Odaimoku

Daimoku is a Japanese word meaning the title of a sutra. In Nichiren Shoshu Buddhism "O," an honorific prefix, is added to the word to create the term *Odaimoku* which means the sacred invocation or chanting of NamuMyōhōRengeKyō, the title of the Lotus Sutra. The essence of the entire sutra is contained in its title. Therefore, chanting *Odaimoku* is equivalent to chanting the entire sutra. The chanting of *Odaimoku* is the primary practice, because NamuMyōhōRengeKyō is the *Mystic Law* and the Buddha-nature.

Namu is derived from Sanskrit, meaning devotion or dedication with one's whole life. *Myō* means mystic. *Ho* means Law. *Ren* means cause; *Ge* means effect. *Kyō* means teaching or sutra. Simply speaking this phrase means devotion with one's whole life to the teaching of the *Mystic Law* of cause and effect.

Since NamuMyōhōRengeKyō is both the seed and the fruit of Buddhahood, Nichiren Daishonin wrote, "When with our mouths we chant the Mystic Law, our Buddha-nature, being summoned, will invariably emerge."[22] This

---

[22] "How Those Initially Aspiring to the Way Can Attain Buddhahood through the Lotus Sutra," *The Major Writings of*

means that if one chants NamuMyōhōRengeKyō only one time, one is guaranteed enlightenment because the cause has been made that at once sets into motion the realization of Buddhahood at some point, now or in the future.

Gongyo

Gongyo is a conversation between oneself and the Buddha. It is the recitation of the 2nd and 16th chapters of the Lotus Sutra. This is the liturgy of Nichiren Shoshu Buddhism.

Shakyamuni's Lotus Sutra has 28 chapters. So why do we recite only the 2nd and the 16th chapters and no other? The Lotus Sutra is divided in two significant parts. The first 14 chapters contain the theoretical teachings; the second 14 chapters contain the essential or true teachings. The most important chapter of the theoretical teachings is chapter two, entitled "Tactfulness" (*Hoben-pon*). This chapter teaches that everything in the universe is equal, no life form is superior to any other life form, and that not only human beings can be saved, but all living things have the same

Nichiren Daishonin, (Nichiren Shoshu International Center, Tokyo, 1990) Vol. Six, p. 208.

potential to realize enlightenment. It also explains the only reason why Buddhas appear in the world, which is to open, show, awaken and cause all living beings to enter the Buddha's wisdom.

Of the essential teachings, it is chapter sixteen, entitled "The Life-span of the Tathagata"[23] (*Juryo-hon*), which is the most important. This chapter explains why all life is equal. It reveals that the state of Buddhahood is eternal; that all states of existence have always existed in infinite Buddhahood, and Buddhahood has always been present in all the infinite states of existence.

One might assume that the language of *Gongyo* is Japanese because it sounds like Japanese, but it is not. Japanese language speakers have as much difficulty understanding *Gongyo* as non-Japanese speakers. That is because the liturgy of Nichiren Shoshu is actually not in one language. It is a compilation of languages, reflecting the path Buddhism took as it traveled from India through Central Asia to China to Korea to Japan.

The Lotus Sutra itself was an oral conversation between the Buddha and the people. In India during

---

[23] Tathagata – a Sanskrit word that is an honorific title of the Buddha.

Shakyamuni Buddha's time, there were many different tribes of people, all speaking their own languages, and all illiterate because systems of writing had not yet been established. The only means of communication was orally. The only means of learning was by sound—by hearing it and by rote. Immediately after the Buddha's passing, the most scholarly Buddhist monks came together to compile the teachings. These monks were from the various tribes of India, and China and other outlying countries. Each one would begin his statement by saying, "Thus I heard," and then recite the sound in their own language or dialect that they heard the Buddha speak. The monks in the assembly would either concur or amend. The sutra was compiled by sounds and not by words in a painstaking manner, eventually confirmed by hundreds of monks, and carefully passed down from generation to generation in just such a way.

The Lotus Sutra was transcribed only after a system of writing had been developed. Monks and priests ultimately came to a consensus on what the Buddha had said and how it should be written. They wrote the sutra to suit the sounds that the Buddha conveyed using phonetics, which they decided was the best way to create proximate sounds. This process of transcribing the sounds—not words—took a thousand years.

It is not known what the first language of the Lotus Sutra was since there is no record of the original language. Most likely it was written in one of the local dialects of Central Asia, and later formalized into Sanskrit. Then as early as 255 C.E. the first Chinese translation was made. As the Lotus Sutra was transmitted from country to country, words were added, subtracted or compounded by pairing a Sanskrit prefix with a Chinese suffix, as an example.

The Nichiren Shoshu liturgy recited today—the 2nd and 16th chapters—is derived from a Chinese translation of the Lotus Sutra made in 406 C.E. by Kumarajiva, a Central Asian Buddhist monk and scholar. The liturgy consists of Chinese characters with Japanese pronunciation, which has further been phonetically transcribed into the various languages of the world. Therefore, no matter what the native language of the speaker, the sound of *Gongyo* is virtually the same. Thus, the language of *Gongyo* is universal.

In one sense, it would seem as it has been established above, that *Gongyo* and *Ōdaimoku* are not in one language. However, on the other hand, they *are* in one language. They are in the Buddha's language, and they cannot be chanted in any other language. For they are in *the language of the heart*. Our mind may not understand the words, but our heart does. And it is nourishment for the heart.

Gongyo must be recited sincerely. When *Gongyo* is recited slowly, or at a reasonable pace, one feels one's own Buddha-nature. One feels the peace of mind and joy of the sutra. It's important that one puts one's heart into *Gongyo*, because, after all, it is a personal conversation between the individual and the Buddha.

Inherent in the rhythm of *Gongyo* is the spirit of all that *Gongyo* is supposed to be. If *Gongyo* is not done at a reasonable pace, pronouncing every word, one cannot feel the Buddha-nature.

Centuries ago, when *Gongyo* was first established, there were no metronomes to keep a consistent rhythm. The sound of the rainfall— the consistent tat – tat – tat – tat – tat of the falling rain was used to set the rhythm. It was not the words so much as the rhythm that was learned. Once the rhythm was mastered the sounds came. The sounds were matched to the rhythm. The meanings of the words are not the focus; it is the sound.

Why do we need to do *Gongyo* if the Ōdaimoku is the essence of the entire sutra? Because *Gongyo* is like an instruction manual while the *Ōdaimoku* (NamuMyōhōRengeKyō) is the actual device, the crucial element, the thing itself. We need the instruction manual to know how to put the device together and how to operate it. We need to be reminded every day that we have Buddha-nature, and how to behave as a Buddha.

Gohonzon

Gongyo and *Ōdaimoku* are chanted to a mandala called Gohonzon.

Gohonzon is a piece of rice paper or wood representing the Law. The Law, however, is not the paper. Looking at the front of Gohonzon one sees the *kanji* characters of NamuMyōhōRengeKyō. When the Gohonzon is turned over one cannot see the written Law. The Law is neither the front nor the back of Gohonzon; the Law is NamuMyōhōRengeKyō. But to see *MyōhōRengeKyō* is difficult. When one looks at a mirror one thinks one is looking at oneself, but it is only an image of one's physical self that one is viewing. We cannot see inside ourselves— our thoughts, or our spiritual aspect. Gohonzon is the mirror of our heart—a window to our soul. We need to see inside our soul. We need a mirror so that we know what we look like in our heart.

Unlike travel on this earth where, if you travel east you will go on until you arrive where you started, in Nichiren Daishonin's Buddhism if you travel east you will go on forever. Thus, Gohonzon represents all physical phenomena and spiritual phenomena in the universe, across the three time periods of past, present and future. These elements are also written on Gohonzon.

Each human life is also included in the universe. The Gohonzon is a small scroll that represents all aspects of life. Down the center of Gohonzon is written the Law of NamuMyōhōRengeKyō. It is this Law which governs everything including the protective forces of Buddhism (often referred to as Buddhist gods). Because NamuMyōhōRengeKyō encompasses everything, including ourselves, we are not searching for Buddha or gods outside ourselves. We must realize that we have Buddha-nature within us, and Buddha-nature is one of the elements that is common to everything.

The most significant aspect of Gohonzon is *NamuMyōhōRengeKyō-Nichiren,* which is written down the center. Everything else that appears on Gohonzon is secondary. As Gohonzon is the representation of the Law at the center of all life, which enlightens all Buddhas, Gohonzon must be handled with the same care that one has for oneself.

Jigyō Keta

Jigyō keta is the practice of Nichiren Shoshu Buddhism. *Jigyō* means that one seeks enlightenment for oneself by practicing the True Law. *Keta* means one seeks enlightenment for others by teaching them and enlightening them to the True Law.

There is no distinction between oneself and others. Just as fish are inseparable from the water in which they swim, so too are man and his environment inseparable. Man's environment consists of everything around him that is not him, including other people he comes in contact with. Moreover, since man cannot become enlightened in a vacuum—he cannot become enlightened unless his environment also becomes enlightened—it is necessary for man to enlighten his environment for he himself to become enlightened. One person's enlightenment is dependent on the enlightenment of others. Therefore, practicing for others—that is, the practice of leading others to enlightenment—is just as important as seeking enlightenment for oneself. *Jigyō* and *keta* are of equal value. There is no greater gift that one can give another than the Law of NamuMyōhōRengeKyō.

The *keta* practice—telling others about NamuMyōhōRengeKyō—is also known as *shakubuku*.

IV

Elements of Practice

These elements are the environment we create to do our twice-daily practice.

The Altar

In Nichiren Shoshu Buddhism, the altar is the place of practice in one's home or in a temple. As mentioned earlier, it is a place free of evil. It consists of a cabinet, in which the Gohonzon is enshrined, and a table or altar, which is placed in front of the cabinet. On the altar is placed either a single candle on the right side, a vase of green leaves on the left side and an incense burner in the center, or two candles and two vases of greens, one of each placed on either side.

Every element on the altar is an expression of offering to Gohonzon, and a reflection of one's faith. To receive the true benefit of the practice of Nichiren Daishonin's Buddhism, it is important to uphold the traditions of practice as directed. As Daishonin himself explained, "Whether you chant the Buddha's name, recite the sutra or merely offer flowers and incense, all your virtuous acts will implant benefits and good fortune in your life. With this conviction you should put your faith into practice."[24]

---

[24] "On Attaining Buddhahood," *The Major Writings of Nichiren Daishonin* (Nichiren Shoshu International Center, Tokyo, 1979), Vol. One, p. 4.

Green Leaves

Evergreens are offered to Gohonzon as they are symbolic of eternal life. The formal name of the evergreens is *shikimi*, and is similar to mountain laurel.

Pretty, colorful flowers express the transient states of vitality and decline. When flowers are in bloom they express beauty, robustness and vigor, the vital aspects of life. When flowers die, they look ugly and have a foul smell—the declining aspect of life—and the foul smell permeates the air, making flowers unsuitable as an offering to Gohonzon. The fleeting beauty of a flower represents impermanence and uncertainty. By contrast, evergreens, being green in all seasons, express the eternity of the *Mystic Law* (*Myōhō*) and the life of all living things. Additionally, the *shikimi*, itself, is both an evergreen and an aromatic tree.

At the time Buddhism was imported to Japan from China by way of Korea, the only evergreen in Japan was the aromatic *shikimi*, which was green all year round. Pretty, colorful flowers came to appear in the markets of villages and towns only after Japan opened up to trading with other countries. Therefore, the *shikimi* was offered to Gohonzon because it was available year around, even in the cold season. Today, any non-flowering green leaves are offered.

Candles

Candles represent death. They also symbolize the Buddha's wisdom which illuminates the darkness of the world of death. White candles are used rather than colored candles as they signify purity.

Incense

Incense represents the Middle Way between the worlds of life and death. Thus, it represents the reality of the Buddha's life. Because it is an aromatic tree, the *shikimi* is also used as an ingredient in incense sticks. Although *shikimi* eventually withers and dies, its scent remains, which is also an expression of eternal life. Even if the fire in the stick of incense goes out, the scent lingers in the room. This too is an expression of eternal life.

The *shikimi* incense, which is symbolic of the realm of life, is lit with the flame of a candle, symbolic of the realm of death, and burnt in an incense burner. The blending of the realms of life and death represent the Middle Way.[25] The fragrance of the incense purifies the air in front of the Gohonzon.

Three sticks of incense are usually offered. This symbolizes the Three Treasures: the Buddha, the Law and the Priest. However, if one cannot burn three sticks of incense because the smell is too harsh, it is acceptable to burn just one.

Water

Water is the source of life. Offer a cup of water every morning before breakfast, keeping it uncovered during morning *Gongyo* and during the rest of the day. Before evening *Gongyo*, empty the water cup and put the cover back on. If the water cup does not have a cover, turn the cup upside down. The Sanskrit word for water is *arghah*. This is the root from which the Latin word "aqua" was derived. As it is so hot in India, it is the custom to serve water to an honored guest. This is how the custom of offering water to

---

[25] *The Middle Way* – life is neither existence nor non-existence, the reality of life is that it is both. It is the mystic entity of *MyōhōRengeKyō* that is the reality of all things.

the Buddha arose. Water is the most valuable offering to the Gohonzon, therefore it is customary to place it higher than the other elements of the altar.

Other Offerings

In "The Gift of Rice"[26] Nichiren Daishonin wrote, "...Life itself is the most precious of all treasures. Even the treasures of the entire universe cannot equal the value of a single human life. Life is like a lamp, and food like oil. When the oil is gone, the flame will die out, and without food, life will cease." Thus, in Japan cooked rice and fruit are placed on the altar as an offering to the Buddha. The grain does not have to be rice. It should be whatever the individual eats: oatmeal, toast, granola, etc. A small amount of grain is offered in the morning, and is placed next to the water. It should be removed after morning *Gongyo* and eaten. Fresh fruit is placed in a bowl, and placed on the altar. It should be eaten before it becomes over-ripe.

The offerings of grains and fruit express the attitude

---

[26] "The Gift of Rice," *The Major Writings of Nichiren Daishonin*, Nichiren Shoshu International Center, Tokyo, 1979),Vol. One, p.267

of sustaining the life of the Buddha.

Bell

Just as incense represents an offering of fragrance to the Buddha, ringing the bell represents an offering of music. For this reason, it should be struck in a way that is aesthetically pleasing to the person who is doing *Gongyo*.

Traditionally, priests ring the bell as follows: the bell is not rung during the first prayer. For the second prayer, ring the bell seven times before the recitation of the 2nd *(Hoben)* chapter. Ring the bell three times at the end of the 2nd chapter. And ring the bell seven times at the beginning of Ōdaimoku. Ring the bell five times to conclude Ōdaimoku.

Lay believers should respect the tradition, but it is not necessary to strike the bell an exact number of times.

Prayer Beads

We call the prayer beads *juzu*. The *juzu* represent the Law. The beads are perfectly round. Their roundness symbolizes the mystical cycle of life and the universe. The *juzu* consist of 108 beads of equal size in the body of the *juzu*, which represent 108 sufferings and desires of human existence. There are an additional four smaller beads strung within the 108 beads, which represent the Four Great Bodhisattvas (Jōgyō, Muhengyō, Jyogyō, and Anryugyō), signifying the four noble qualities of true self, eternity, purity and happiness, respectively. It was predicted that after the 2000 years following Shakyamuni's passing, the four bodhisattvas would spread the Law of NamuMyōhōRengeKyō. That is why Nichiren Daishonin is so important. He was the first to introduce the Law and propagate it some 2,200 years after Shakyamuni's passing.

The two large beads at each end of the *juzu* indicate the two Buddhas, Tahō[27] and Shakyamuni, who represent two parents, as well as the principles of reality (all phenomena) and wisdom (the Law), respectively.

To hold the prayer beads correctly, place the end with two tassels on the middle finger of the left hand, twist the beads once in the middle and place the end with the three tassels on the middle finger of the right hand. Put your palms together and place them in front of your chest. The

---

[27] Tahō – Many Treasures Buddha. He is a Buddha who appears in chapter 11 of the Lotus Sutra to lend credence to Shakyamuni's teaching of the Law.

juzu are twisted once so that they don't slip out of your hands. The *juzu* represent the body, but their shape was not intended to suggest the shape of the human body. That idea was added later.

When we put beads on our hands and put our palms together in prayer position, the beads clothe our sufferings and desires. That is the duty of the *juzu*, to envelop our delusions inside our palm. We have worries, anxieties, passions, our minds are constantly troubled, and that is why we carry beads.

The *juzu* are as important as the Gohonzon[28]. Don't put them on the floor. Don't play with them as toys. Don't wear them, or use them as ornamentation. Even though we use our hands to hold them and touch them, we must handle them respectfully. If they are broken, even a little, some people may fix them and continue using them, but they should not do that.

If someone were to put the *juzu* in his or her hands, even though he or she did not believe in Nichiren Shoshu Buddhism, such a person would have the same potential as

---

[28] Gohonzon – the true object of worship representing the universal Law and Buddha-nature in all things, NamuMyōhōRengeKyō.

a believer to become enlightened. That is because all life is equal.

V

Holidays

The most important religious holidays in Nichiren Shoshu are *Oeshiki, Risshu, Oko* and New Years. In addition, the national holidays (not religious holidays) of the country in which believers live are also celebrated. For example, in the United States believers celebrate Thanksgiving, the 4th of July, Memorial Day, Labor Day, birthdays, anniversaries, Mother's and Father's Day, etc.

Oeshiki

October 13

Oeshiki is the most important ceremony in Nichiren Shoshu. It is a celebration of the eternal life of Nichiren Daishonin as well as our own eternal life.

On the 13th day of the 10th month in the 5th year of *Koan* (1282), Nichiren Daishonin's body, which was the same as any human body, passed away at the age of 61. Nevertheless, the Buddha-nature within Daishonin's life and all life—the life of NamuMyōhōRengeKyō itself—did not die. It never dies; it is eternal. That is why we celebrate Oeshiki: to affirm the eternal life of the Buddha.

At the time the Daishonin passed away, the 13th day of the 10th month, according to the lunar calendar, would have actually fallen at the end of November rather than in October. It would have been late fall or even wintery then. Yet, throughout Japan the cherry blossoms bloomed. So for Oeshiki, paper cherry blossoms are made and placed on either side of Gohonzon.

Oeshiki is a festive day. Believers gather together on October 13th for a great celebration to honor the occasion. It is a day when Buddhism is discussed, gifts are exchanged and special foods are prepared. Oeshiki is as important to Nichiren Shoshu Buddhism as Christmas is to Christianity. The intent of the Oeshiki holiday is to celebrate the eternal Buddha-nature, and remind us that it is ever-present.

Oko

13th of Every Month

Because Nichiren Daishonin passed away on the 13th day of the month, we express our appreciation to Daishonin with the *Oko* ceremony on the 13th day of every month to remind us that the Buddha's life is eternal.

Rikkyo-kai-shu-é

April 28

This is the celebration of the "founding of the religion." On this day, the 28th day of the 4th month in the year 1253, Nichiren Daishonin taught, for the first time, that NamuMyōhōRengeKyō is the center of everything. "é" at the end of *Rikkyo-kai-shu*-é means "gathering." People gather on this day to celebrate the day Nichiren established the practice of NamuMyōhōRengeKyō as the True Religion.

New Year's Day

January 1

Nichiren Daishonin wrote, "New Year's Day marks the first day, the first month, the beginning of the year and the start of spring. A person who celebrates this day will gain virtue and be loved by all, just as the moon becomes full gradually, moving from west to east, and the sun shines more brightly traveling from east to west."[29] This day is celebrated because it represents the eternal cycle of renewal.

---

[29] "The New Year's Gosho," *The Major Writings of Nichiren Daishonin* (Nichiren Shoshu International Center, Tokyo. 1979), Vol. One, pp.279

VI

Other Concepts and Thoughts
from
Reverend Raidō Hirota

How the practice of Nichiren Shoshu Buddhism is applied and experienced in daily life.

The Purpose of Life

The essence of Nichiren Daishonin's teachings is not to transcend the four phases of life – birth, old age, sickness and death – but to realize that these four phases are reality. The objective of this practice is not to achieve an existence apart from birth, old age, sickness and death, but to recognize and be mindful of life and what the reality of life is. This is enlightenment. When Shakyamuni Buddha achieved enlightenment, this is what he perceived. He awakened to the realities of life. He did not perceive that life should be happy. He did not realize a condition or emotion beyond the human condition. Enlightenment is, as he perceived, here in this moment, whatever condition we are in, wherever we are. This is the purpose of life: to recognize enlightenment wherever we are.

What is important is to have NamuMyōhōRengeKyō and the True Teachings of Nichiren Daishonin as the basis of our life, and to live our life accordingly. All else is external an unimportant.

Buddhahood Exists Within the Heart

The human body discharges germs and dead cells every day. That is why we have to bathe every day. The anxiety in our life is like the germs on our body. Just as we cannot entirely remove the germs, we cannot remove our anxiety completely; life produces worries and problems as we live it. Enlightenment = having the Buddha's mind. Anxiety = uncleanness. Our life is a constant cycle of these two states—enlightenment and anxiety. This is the truth, the whole truth and nothing but the truth. People alternate between enlightenment and delusion throughout their entire lives.

Only the Lotus Sutra teaches us how to attain supreme enlightenment. The key element is your heart. I can say that concentrating on your heart, finding your teacher in your heart and calling it NamuMyōhōRengeKyō is the best way to attain enlightenment. So, develop sincere faith in NamuMyōhōRengeKyō. Buddhahood is not the result of study and practice, but the state of studying and practicing. Buddhahood does not exist outside your heart, it can only be found within your heart.

If you find a doctrine which leads you to a spiritual realization outside of your heart, it is not a true doctrine.

Both the realization and the doctrine itself are insignificant. Only NamuMyōhōRengeKyō brings us to the true spiritual state of Buddhahood or enlightenment. To call your heart and mind NamuMyōhōRengeKyō is synonymous with Buddhahood. Therefore, you must keep and strengthen your belief in NamuMyōhōRengeKyō. And once again I say, Buddhahood is not the result of study and practice; it is the act of studying and practicing. Buddhahood does not exist outside your heart.

Enlightenment

You may think that the condition or state of Buddhahood does not enter into your mind, and that it is unrealistic to think that you can experience Buddha in your life. That is not at all the case. Deep, deep joy is a very real feeling that you may have experienced. But when I chant in front of Gohonzon, sometimes I am overcome with a feeling of appreciation coming from deep within myself. That feeling is probably the nature of Buddha, or the closest to enlightenment that I have experienced.

Buddhahood is not a concrete thing, nor something that everyone experiences in exactly the same way. It is difficult to describe what enlightenment is as a reality, because it is different for each person. Your experience will depend on who you are and what the situation is. The life condition of Buddha can come in all kinds of forms, all kinds of feelings, all kinds of realizations. When you find some kind of standard you can rely on, then you might be able to judge when you are experiencing the life of Buddha, or what the life condition of Buddha should be.

Enlightenment does not have a fixed form. It cannot be explained as a discrete entity. Nichiren Daishonin explains it like this in his writing, "The Three Kinds of Treasure": "More valuable than treasures in the storehouse are treasures of the body, and the treasures of the heart are the most valuable of all. From the time you read this letter on, strive to accumulate the treasures of the heart."[30] Treasures of the storehouse are money, jewels, property. Treasures of the body are education, social status, and attractive appearance. Treasures of the heart are when you recognize that you have the Buddha-nature of *NamuMyōhōRengeKyō* within you. Even if it is for only one second that you have this feeling or realization, that is

---

[30] "The Three Kinds of Treasure," *The Major Writings of Nichiren Daishonin*, (Nichiren Shoshu International Center, Tokyo, 1981), Vol. Two, p. 279.

enlightenment.

Life and Death

When we human beings look at life and death they seem different. But from the point of view of Nichiren Daishonin, life and death are the same condition; there is no difference between the two. If you look at the eyes of a human being before and after death, you notice a difference; that a change has taken place—a change from life to death. With the human body, there is a definite difference between life and death. But the essence of life never changes, not even in death. It is constant. It is always the same. In death there is life, and in life there is death (fingernails, hair, dead skin). The spirit, however, never dies; even in death the spirit is alive. And of course, in life it is alive.

The human body can be compared to a bottle of water. The form is there and the content is there. If the body dies it would be as if the bottle fell over and the water spilled out. This water is never going to return to the way it was. Water is water. It runs down mountains to the ocean, evaporates and becomes gas, condenses and becomes rain or snow on the mountains, then flows back down to the ocean. It's a cycle. The property of water—H_2O—never changes. But never again will it be the same water—the same river, the same ocean. The essence of water is NamuMyōhōRengeKyō. When water changes form, its essence stays the same. The same is true of human beings. Humans change form, but their essence never changes. It will always be NamuMyōhōRengeKyō.

The sutras expounded before the Lotus Sutra addressed only the life of human beings. With the Lotus Sutra came the teaching that humans cannot exist without the environment. Humans live within air, water, earth, and light. Humans exist within the environment of these four elements. Without these four elements, and without other forms of life, humans could not exist. The Lotus Sutra shows us that other things are essential for our existence. Without these other things, we would not exist. We connect with the environment, that is why we are living at this moment. So, when you talk about the enlightenment of human beings, you must include the environment in that enlightenment. Everything in the entire universe must be included in your enlightenment.

Let's take fish for example. People eat fish. Once eaten, the fish is no longer a fish; it becomes a part of a human being. Man cannot become enlightened if the fish does not become enlightened. When a person breathes in air, the air becomes a part of that person. The air has to become enlightened if man is to become enlightened. Are we humans so superior that we can live without air?

In Buddhism, there is a principle called *ichinen sanzen*.[31] When I am the "single life entity" (*ichinen*) everyone else, as well as the environment, are "all phenomena" or everything (*sanzen*). When someone else is the "single life entity" (*ichinen*), I and everyone else, including the environment, are "all phenomena" (*sanzen*). Life alternates between *ichinen* and *sanzen* (the single life entity and all phenomena). The Lotus Sutra is the first scripture to reveal this concept. Each one of us is a little piece of the whole fabric of life. If it weren't for "all phenomena" (*sanzen*), each one of us would not exist. There is no difference between all the molecules of our body and the environment around us. We are the environment and the environment is us. We are the single life entity and all phenomena. All life is a part of the same thing.

There is only one source of life. That source is NamuMyōhōRengeKyō. NamuMyōhōRengeKyō is *ichinen*

---

[31] Ichinen Sanzen – a single life moment contains three thousand realms of existence, or more simply *ichinen* equals a single life and *sanzen* equals everything.

sanzen. NamuMyōhōRengeKyō comprises everything. It is everything. It is all that there ever was…all that there ever will be. It has always been, and it always will be. Life has never come from any other source. NamuMyōhōRengeKyō is permanent and constant. It is only the form of NamuMyōhōRengeKyō which changes.

Aging and Dying

Life, without exception, consists of the four sufferings: birth, aging, sickness and death. You cannot stop or turn back time – though there are religions, including some Buddhist denominations, which say we can escape from the four sufferings. According to these religions, if you cannot escape the four sufferings, your faith is not strong enough. Nonetheless, it is a universal truth that all life exists with the four sufferings. You must accept this and not be upset by it. Don't run away from it or deny it. No matter how much your health declines, you must come to live with the awareness that the life of Buddha – *NamuMyōhōRengeKyō* – is within you. The physical body will decline, but the life of the Mystic Law, *Myoho*, which is always inside you, will never decline. Even though you may lose your memory, there's no barrier to the Buddha's life. Even though the body dies, the Buddha's life is never-ending.

Human beings' greatest weakness is the fear of dying. Many religions take advantage of this weakness, with some saying if you believe in God, you will not die, or your sickness will be healed and your health restored. Some may say you can be revived after death. Some even keep the dead body in their homes. There are cults which believe such things. Then there is cryopreservation – freezing a dead body soon after death in the hopes that in the future it can be thawed and revived. This is an attempt to change the concept of death, or to deny death.

Nichiren Daishonin says in "The Importance of the Moment of Death,"[32] "First, learn and brace yourself for the fact that a human being will die someday without fail. Then, learn other facets of life."

Most people in this world, from the time of childhood, loathe death; recoil from death; fear death; and are unwilling to accept or acknowledge death. They assume

---

[32] *The Writings of Nichiren Daishonin*, Vol. 2 p. 759

that it's all over when you die.

Learning and bracing yourself for death is not something grim or ominous. To the contrary, it's a way for us to take notice of how precious this life that we have received is. This is something we should learn from a young age. Don't lie, don't steal, don't bully, study hard… these should not be the only guidelines given in life. Believing that, "As long as I'm having a good time and doing fine right now, I'm cool," – is not the way to live. What we need to teach at a young age is that, "Because our lifetime is short, we have to live right."

Because there is a limit to life, life is as important and as precious as a treasure. If there were no limitations, no one would think a great deal of it. If you knew that you would not die, even if you were being reckless, no one would pay attention to safety or health. No one would put any effort into living. Because you will die someday, the time you are alive becomes important. Because there is a goodbye, meeting another being is important. However, death is not the end of a life. It is a passage through to eternal life.

Nichiren Daishonin also wrote, "The exhaled breath never waits for the inhaled one…. Whether one is wise or foolish, old or young, one never knows what will happen to one from one moment to the next". [33]

Exhaled air leaves your body without your effort, just as air expels from a balloon. The exhaled air is a breath of death. The inhaled air needs strength for the body to live, so it is a breath of life.

The last breath a human being takes ends with an exhaled air. A person dies because he did not have the strength to take a breath. In other words, living things live by connecting the breath of life and the breath of death from moment to moment. But, there is no guarantee that the breath of life will always come after the breath of death. The Buddha's teaching tells us that we should be conscious of the fact that all of us are always living back to back with life and death.

If a person thinks that life is all about the time one is alive, then for that person death would fundamentally be suffering. Thinking this way would elicit the feeling that there is no place to go. It would generate distress and suffering. A person who once was alive stops responding to anything. It is reality that seems like a lie and a dream. What then was existence and relationships about? It is a truth that

---

[33] *The Writings of Nichiren Daishonin,"* Vol. II, p. 759

just can't be reasoned.

Life isn't only about death. To be born, to grow old, to get sick, and to die are life itself. Buddhism teaches us that life is eternal; it has no beginning or end. It is not because I'm a Buddhist that I say this. This is something I truly, genuinely believe.

We think our lives are our own, but life is not something you possess. There are people who think it's their right to live or to kill. That thinking is wrong. The life you have, you are taking under your care. It is a life that you are borrowing. Because it's a life that you are taking care of, or borrowing, there comes a time when you will have to return it.

If you are saddened by death, then you have to value this time that you are alive. While you are alive, you have to find out why you were born, why you are alive. Nichiren Daishonin says that there is nothing more regrettable than not realizing that your human life hosts the same life of NamuMyōhōRengeKyō as does the most precious life—that of Buddha.

The teaching says that at the root of every moment in life and death, there is the life of NamuMyōhōRengeKyō. All sentient beings in this world are connected. There is no life that is not connected to one another.

The life of human beings, stones (minerals), plants, animals, insects, earth, water, fire, air, light… and so on are connected. Your life is supported by those connections. The entirety becomes One Life. We think that billions of living organisms exist on this earth independently, but Buddha's view is that this One Life consists of all life connections, including every life form that exists beyond this earth.

Death is a transformation within the One Life. So, the one life that contains so many connected lives isn't the one that died. The One Life continues to live and to exist eternally. Even when the end of the earth comes, the existence of the totality of the connected life – the One Life – remains the same. For example, the cherry blossoms of last year's cherry tree fell to the ground. Would you say that the cherry tree died? Just as it did last year, the cherry tree blossomed again this year. They might look the same, but there is not even one blossom on that tree that is the same as the others. The transformation occurs based on the cherry tree – the life totality.

Farewell is a lament and a sorrow, as if the world had ended. However, the One Life (the connected life) does not end. It is not the end of the world. The One Life is eternal. That is what Nichiren Daishonin taught. Make this point your foundation, and practice it on a routine basis. See your life objectively, and ask yourself: Am I living my life in a way that I will not regret it should I die at this moment?

We are counseled to always see our own life objectively. Learn from Nichiren Daishonin's teaching regarding what life is about, and overcome your angst and sorrows.

There is no Difference Between Any Living Thing

Every living thing can achieve enlightenment because all life itself is NamuMyōhōRengeKyō. Everything possesses the life of Buddha. Because the Buddha's life is in you, when you chant NamuMyōhōRengeKyō, which is the Buddha's life, you awaken it. Before the Lotus Sutra was taught, even if all society wanted to practice True Buddhism it would have been difficult to do so, and impossible for women. Society was patriarchal—men were dominant. The role of women was to support the men and do as they were told. Women had no power or free will to determine their own lives. That is the kind of society into which true Buddhism was introduced. Even today, there are cultures and societies that are still like this. In the 12th chapter of the Lotus Sutra, however, it is revealed that even animals and women can become enlightened. This teaching was revolutionary. There is no way that men and only men can achieve enlightenment and the rest of life cannot. All life has the same value and the same potential. Therefore, only NamuMyōhōRengeKyō can save all life – women, animals, plants, everything. Only the practice of NamuMyōhōRengeKyō can enlighten all life.

In front of Gohonzon there is no difference between any living thing. There is no higher or lower being, no higher or lower status. No discrimination between life forms, whether you are old or young, male or female, human, animal or plant. To believe this is to practice True Buddhism.

Reincarnation and Karma

What happens in life is 50% karma, and 50% free will.

Many Buddhist sutras teach about people dying and being reborn as someone else. There are many examples in the sutras and in the writings of Nichiren Daishonin[34] where Shakyamuni speaks of his previous lives. For instance, in one of his previous lives he was born as Bodhisattva Jofukyō[35], and at another time as Sessen Doji.[36] When we hear these stories we may think, "I, myself will reincarnate as this particular person." But I don't think that's the case.

Someone asked me whether the butterflies which appeared emerging out of the rubble of the World Trade Center a month after 9/11 were an incarnation of the human beings who had died on 9/11. To be honest, as a human being, I don't know if they were or not.

Back in the 13th century, during Nichiren Daishonin's time, there were three farmers from Atsuhara Village who were persecuted for being followers of the Daishonin. They were eventually beheaded by the government for their beliefs. Their lives disappeared from this world, but their spirits merged into the greater universe, which includes all physical aspects of the universe as well as all spiritual, unseen aspects of the universe within the three time periods of past, present and future. In

---

[34] The writings of Nichiren Daishonin – the Buddhist term is *gosho*.
[35] Bodhisattva Jofukyō – (or Fukyō) Bodhisattva Never Despise whose story appears in the 20th Chapter of the Lotus Sutra.
[36] Sessen Doji – a hermit who in practicing austerities in pursuit of enlightenment encountered a demon who taught him the Law.

Buddhism, this "greater universe" is known as *sanzen daisen sekai*. The lives of the three farmers fused with this greater universe, and from there manifested into a different form of life. That different form of life could be human or any other form of life. This is Nichiren Daishonin's teaching of the disappearance and manifestation of life.

There is not a direct linkage between one person dying and another person appearing; it is more dynamic than that. One life disappears, merges into the life of the greater universe, and then from the greater universe another life will re-form and appear as a human being.

When we die and disappear from this physical world and merge into the universe, we lose our identity as a particular life form, a particular shape, a particular color, a particular smell, etc. Everything disappears and our spirit merges into the greater universe. This is a difficult concept to explain, but here is an example: If I were to smash a cookie, it would disintegrate into small, tiny particles which we call atoms and molecules. The same would happen if we were to smash, let's say a radio. If we smashed a radio, it would also be reduced to atoms and molecules, as well. Can the atoms resulting from the smashing of the radio and the atoms resulting from the smashing of the cookie be distinguished, one from the other? I would have to say, no.

Likewise, the particles that compose the form of one human being or an object will merge into the universe and lose their individual identity. Hence no longer will I have the identity of myself, and no longer will you have the identity of who you are in this life.

One might wonder how karma figures into all of this. Karma consists of many, many, factors. Karma is not just you in isolation. Many components make us who we are, such as parents, family, society, country, history, etc. The same is true of karma. I am one member of a family. Being a member of a particular family contributes one type of karma to me. A cluster of karmas makes us who we are.

Or one may ask what about collective karma as opposed to individual karma?

Even though we use such terms as "collective karma" and "individual karma", there are not clear lines between the two. In terms of what we call *ichinen sanzen*, it all comes down to one large entity of karma. Individual karma can be considered as part of it.

Let me explain further. If you are in a family, you look at other members of your family and say, "That's my family." Another member of your family looks at you and the other members and says, "That's my family." In that sense the individual and the collective or the whole are indistinguishable. Yet all your combined factors make you very unique. The same can be said of karma.

The lives of different individuals merge into the universe without discrimination between believers of Nichiren Shoshu Buddhism and non-believers, or how one lived in a previous life. We all merge into a collective whole. If we approached our daily prayer from Daishonin's perspective, our attitude would be that we want to positively influence others. It is not our aspiration to make a distinction between those who chant and those who do not, with the attitude that those who chant are superior to others. We are all the same. When we chant, we are not chanting just for ourselves. We are chanting for others to chant with us so that the power we gain from chanting can be shared with others. The intention being that when we all fuse into the greater universe, the collective whole will have a greater infusion of NamuMyōhōRengeKyō.

We all live in this society as individuals and have points of view different from one another. NamuMyōhōRengeKyō, which we chant, is so powerful that it can influence not only the limited environment in which we live, but can influence the entire universe. One may not necessarily want to merge into a collective group with others, but each of us has enough power to influence others. We don't have to be influenced by others; we can be more dynamic than others and thus influence them. NamuMyōhōRengeKyō is more influential than anything.

That entity that is the core of our hearts, the core of our lives is the thing that connects each of us to the life of Buddha when we chant NamuMyōhōRengeKyō to Gohonzon. For instance, sometimes we may feel that we don't want to do *Gongyo* but we do it anyway. Because we do it, our lives begin to feel energized. That feeling comes about because the core of our hearts has been activated and energized as a result of connecting to Gohonzon. That life or that core, which I am attempting to describe, unfortunately cannot be described in a succinct way. That's why I made reference to atoms and molecules. The core of our hearts is an intangible. That feeling of being energized is the feeling we want to achieve when we chant. We chant to become closer to the Buddha in our hearts.

Causes and Conditions

In Buddhism, all matter is believed to be composed of the five elements: earth, water, fire, wind, and _ku_[37]. These are known as the "five great elements," and in fact the five-storied pagoda is symbolic of these five elements, which a person is restored to after death.

The word _engi_ is a shortened form of the expression _in-nen sho-ki_. This four-character phrase means that everything has cause and condition. "Cause" (_in_) would be the factors that directly bring about a result. "Condition" (_en_) refers to factors, which complement the primary "cause." The cause (_in_) combined with the condition(s) (_en_) equal karma. A flower is often used as a metaphor to explain this: A flower blooms because seeds are planted and shoots come forth. The seed is the direct cause for the blossoming of the flower. However, flowers will not grow simply from seeds; they must be given water and sunshine. In this instance, water and sunlight are indirect factors causing the flower to bloom, and are therefore, conditions.

Just as a flower is made to bloom because of a "cause"—the seed—and the "conditions"—the water and

---

[37] Ku - air

sunshine—all existence, including ourselves, are not realized independently, but appear as a result of various causes and conditions. Hence, all phenomena are manifested as a result of the mutual relationship of innumerable causes and conditions. *Engi* refers to the fact that when causes and conditions change, the phenomena will also change. Therefore, this suggests "impermanence" (all things arise, change, and are extinguished), and no self (no existence) is absolute and immutable.

To be more specific, human beings are supported by the entire universe. If a person eats a potato, that potato is assimilated into the human body and thus becomes human. Likewise, when a person eats beef, the beef becomes human. That is why we cannot pray for the enlightenment of human beings alone, we must also pray for the enlightenment of all living things. Only the Lotus Sutra teaches enlightenment for all living beings. The coming together of trillions of lives constitutes "all living beings."

It is past karma, which determines the form the five elements will take. That is, whether a being is born human, animal, plant, etc. Each of the five elements has mind or soul. That is to say, earth has mind, water has mind, wind has mind, fire has mind, and air or *ku* has mind. When the causes and conditions determine that the five elements will materialize as a human being, then that being will have a human soul. If it is determined that the five elements will materialize as an animal, then that being will have an animal soul. While alive these beings will do many things, which will engender many causes that will lead to different karma, resulting in different destinies in future lives.

We see plants blooming every day. The flower dies, but still life remains and the plant will blossom again. Yet, there is no person "A" who, after he or she dies, will be reborn as person "A". If person "A" were to be reborn as person "A," he or she would have to have the same parents, live at the same address, have the same classmates and teachers as in this life, otherwise it will not be the same person "A." A man who is a good marksman in this life will not be reborn a good marksman in the next life.

Hate, sadness and love are causes and conditions which impact our karma and determine our destiny. Chanting NamuMyōhōRengeKyō is also a cause and condition which affects our karma. When one dies, the spirit will merge with the universe, but it is not certain where in the universe it will reside. The universe is composed of innumerable lives. These lives have formed connections or relationships from previous lifetimes. Where a spirit comes to reside is determined by its relationship with other lives in the universe, or its relationship with the universe as a whole. For a human being to create a relationship with NamuMyōhōRengeKyō will make a big difference. When one is connected to *MyōhōRengeKyō* it is profound.

The Buddhist Concept of God

From the perspective of monotheistic traditions such as Christianity, Judaism and Islam, God is an absolute, omnipotent, omniscient, authoritative being who created everything. But there is a big difference between the term god, the concept of god and the status of god.

In Buddhism, everything, sentient and insentient, has a god. Even one grain of rice has a god. A mountain and a river have gods. A car, a toilet each have a god. The Buddhist gods are called *shoten zenjin*. In Japanese, the word "god" translates as *kami*. *Jin* of *shoten zenjin* is the same Japanese *kanji* character as *kami*. The original meaning of the *kanji* character for *kami* is "invisible existence." If you look up the word *kami* in a Japanese-English dictionary it would just say "god." But the concept of "god" is so different from the meaning, which is an invisible existence, a spirit, a presence. The words nerve, neurology, psychology in

Japanese all have the same *kanji* character as *kami* because these disciplines deal with something that is not visible, yet exists. So, the concept of *kami* in Japanese and *shoten zenjin* in Buddhism is not the almighty being who created the world – the sky, the earth, the plants, animals, and human beings. The God who created the world is the God of the Bible or Koran. In Buddhism, *kami*, translated as god in English, is an existence whose duty is to protect, to observe, to guard. The Buddhist gods don't create anything. To practice Buddhism, if you are thinking of god in Western terms, you have to change your way of thinking.

Desires are Enlightenment
(*Bonnō Soku Bodai*)

The essential nature of this age is good and evil. Good and evil are as intermingled as milk in coffee. When you add milk to coffee, the milk mixes and becomes inseparable. Desires (*bonnō*) and enlightenment (*bodai*) are the same. They are inseparable. This Buddhist principle is referred to as *bonnō soku bodai* – desires are enlightenment.

A single statement made by an individual can be taken as a great declaration by one person, and an outrageous lie by another person. Just one single statement can be viewed in very different ways.

In his early teachings, Shakyamuni taught that negative thoughts had to be eliminated and, that one needed to purify one's mind to attain enlightenment. But in the Lotus Sutra, taught at the very end of Shakyamuni's teachings, he said there needs to be a law by which anyone can become enlightened, because no one can separate good and evil from one's life. The law, therefore, has to be powerful enough to enlighten life where good and evil co-exist indivisibly.

Shakyamuni illustrated this well in the 12th chapter of the Lotus Sutra. As the story goes, Shakyamuni's cousin, Devadatta[38] was jealous of the Buddha and tried on numerous occasions to kill him and usurp his position. On one occasion, Devadatta tried to roll a boulder on the Buddha to crush him. At another time, he unleashed a wild elephant in an attempt to trample him. While he never succeeded at killing Shakyamuni, Devadatta committed himself to the path of evil until the very last day of his life.

---

[38] Devadatta – In their youth Siddhartha (Shakyamuni) and Devadatta fell in love with the same woman, the beautiful princess Yashodhara. Siddhartha won her hand in marriage. Devadatta never forgave him, hence discord ensued between them.

In the end, while attempting to kill the Buddha with fingernails saturated with snake venom, Devadatta plunged into a crevice in the earth created by a sudden earthquake. Just before he fell, Shakyamuni urged him to take faith. Perhaps out of fear Devadatta tried, but unfortunately only managed to utter, "*Namu*"[39] as he plunged to his death. It is said he went straight to hell. Shakyamuni, with his supernatural powers, visited Devadatta in hell and encouraged him to follow the Law. The Buddha predicted that Devadatta would become Heavenly King Buddha in a future life. And as Heavenly King Buddha, he would live in a world called Heavenly Way and abide there for 20 kalpas.[40]

Shakyamuni's followers were surprised and even angered at Shakyamuni's treatment of Devadatta. Why

---

[39] Namu- devotion

[40] Kalpa – In "Letter to Horen" (*Major Writings* Vol. 7) Nichiren Daishonin defines kalpa as follows. "Suppose that the span of human life is eighty thousand years, and that it decreases one year every hundred years, or ten years every thousand years. Let us suppose that it decreases at this rate until the life span has reached ten years....Then the process would reverse, and after a hundred years, the life span would increase to eleven years, and, after another hundred years to twelve years. After a thousand years, it would have increased to twenty years, and this would continue until it once more reached eighty thousand years. The time required to complete this combined process of decrease and increase is called a kalpa."

would the Buddha try to save Devadatta who, after all, had attempted to kill the Buddha on numerous occasions? This the disciples could not understand. Shakyamuni explained his actions, saying, "Devadatta was my teacher in a past life. Thanks to his guidance I was able to become enlightened. Now I can repay my gratitude to him."

We learn from this that within the three existences of past, present and future, good and evil have an inseparable nature. Thus, it is not just in the present time, it is consistent across the three existences.

There are many, many parables throughout the sutras of Shakyamuni that emphasize this point. Another example is Kishibojin,[41] who had countless children. Although she herself was a mother of many children, she kidnapped the children of other mothers and ate them, or fed them to her own children. Shakyamuni Buddha taught her a lesson by kidnapping and hiding one of her children. Through the agony she suffered from the loss of her own child, Kishibojin came to realize the pain she had inflicted on other parents. From that moment on, she vowed to be a protector of children. As a result, she became a Buddhist

---

[41] Kishibojin – also Kishimojin – the mother-of-devils or the goddess of children. She appears in the 26th chapter of the Lotus Sutra.

god[42], protecting the practitioners of the Lotus Sutra.

There are many stories of transformations from bad to good. Even within the same individual's lifetime there can be actions taken that lead in a completely different direction. So again, there is this indivisible nature of good and evil within our lives.

By the same measure can we view the indivisibility and interrelatedness of our desires and enlightenment. That is the meaning of *bonnō soku bodai* (desires are enlightenment). This concept, that one individual has an inseparable good and evil nature, was only taught in the Lotus Sutra. The idea of "desires are enlightenment" may sound like a contradiction, but it's not. It is a truth.

On Vegetarianism

Vegetables are like people. It is not right to think that you can eat vegetables but not animals. Vegetables, animals, they are all life. If you are concerned about eating a living thing, you have to realize that all things that we need to nourish our bodies are alive or have had life. If you think

---

[42] Buddhist god – *shoten zenjin,* force of nature.

this way, you would have to eliminate everything. There is scientific proof that when a cabbage, for example, is being cut, the cabbage signals telepathically through electric energy that it hurts. A plant has the same life value as an animal. It is wrong to think that you can eat a vegetable, but should not eat an animal, unless it is for medical reasons.

On Omens

In this era in which we live, which is called the Latter Day of the Law or *Mappō*[43], we tend to analyze the cause of natural disasters scientifically. Typhoons or hurricanes, we say are caused by the mixture of winds blowing into areas of warm water and collecting moisture, while colder air moves in below and creates a pressure which causes the winds to swirl and move rapidly. Earthquakes, we say, are the result of the tectonic plates, which make up the earth's crust, shifting, and as they shift, pressure builds up along the fault lines in the earth's crust, which eventually causes a sudden release of stress in the form of shaking on the

---

[43] Mappō – the Latter Day of the Law - the age of decline of the Law; this present time period which began in 1052, about 2000 years after the death of Shakyamuni. It is called the evil age.

surface. Because we cannot prevent these natural disasters from occurring, we respond by cleaning up, and rebuilding.

Long ago, when there were earthquakes, typhoons, lunar eclipses, solar eclipses, and other natural disasters or occurrences, people would turn inward to reflect on their lives. They would question whether they were living correctly, or whether they were living in the wrong way, and thereby causing these disasters to happen. The surrounding natural world provided the context for people to evaluate their way of living and way of thinking. They sensed that their behavior was somehow related to changes in nature.

People of today think that people living long ago were unscientific, naïve, or ignorant, because the people of past eras did not know the causes of the natural disasters, and therefore did not know the reason the strange phenomena occurred. However, people living in the past considered their lives and nature to be connected, and that the relationship between humans and nature could not be separated. They believed that when a person's mind was unstable, perverted or not at ease, it would cause natural disasters. The inverse was also true: if nature was not at peace, that would affect the human mind, causing an imbalance. Thus, when people of earlier eras saw something unusual occurring around them, they believed they had to self-reflect because, as they understood it, life and the environment are inseparable.

I do not agree that people of the past were naïve. People today think that human beings are superior beings with power and knowledge. But it is the people of the past who understood that everything is connected; that if one thing is abnormal or out of order, or acting strange, then everything will reflect that disharmony. Understanding the inseparability or connection of everything, in my opinion, indicates that the mindset of the people of past eras is superior to the mindset, or way of thinking of us living today.

In teaching about NamuMyōhōRengeKyō, Nichiren Daishonin explains that we have to recognize the changes in the environment – in nature – as warnings. They present a chance to reflect on ourselves. We shouldn't only be afraid of these natural disasters. We have to face them head-on and ask ourselves, what are these disasters trying to tell us, or teach us? Rather than viewing natural disasters or unreasonable changes in the environment as something terrible, we must change our thinking to recognize them as an opportunity. This is the teaching of NamuMyōhōRengeKyō taught by Nichiren Daishonin.

In the midst of the COVID-19 pandemic, which has been the cause of death of millions of people worldwide, came new viruses, the Monkey Pox pandemic, wild fires, floods, droughts, earthquakes, volcanic eruptions and warnings of famine. We are living in dark times. People are confused. They had fallen into a dark place due to COVID, and have become increasingly despairing. Living at this time, we have to confront the conditions of human society. We have to face it. We can no longer live the way we have been living. Through the COVID pandemic, and all the other catastrophic events that have transpired in recent years, we are being warned that we must self-reflect.

In the middle of this confused time, the war in Ukraine was launched by Russia. This reminds us of how foolish human beings are. We believe human beings were much wiser than they are. But it simply shows that human beings are cruel beings, lusting for power. With this dynamic power play by one nation, coupled with political power, I cannot imagine where this war is headed. What I have said many times before about the world order, is that a small country must obey the wishes of a big country. They must surrender when a larger country is imposing its will to control the smaller country. If a country has a greater number and more powerful weapons, it will dominate the country that has fewer and less powerful weapons. And a person who has more resources and more money will control the person who has fewer resources and less money. It will benefit one country. This is how the balance of power and the rules in the world are decided. The world has been moving in this direction for a long time, and is now structured this way. This is discrimination. In these confusing times, we must realize what we are living through.

Nichiren Daishonin said everyone, whether weak or strong, has Buddha-life, and all life is equal. In addition to what we consider human rights, we must realize that every life is precious. All life is equal.

The interactions between China and Russia, Iran and Russia, and many other countries which are supporting Russia, are grounded in what each entity, or each person will gain. How the relationships are structured is based on, not whether it is right or wrong, but whether it is beneficial or not. This is how countries are making their decisions. At this time, there are so many lives being taken. Much blood is being spilt. Cruel things are happening because leaders of countries are valuing power and material gain above human life.

We all have to wake up to the fact that there is a limit to how the world is structured and how it is moving. The world is structured around a power dynamic between countries. There is a limit to this kind of power play. We have to realize that this structure is not sustainable. We need to wake up to this fact. The situation is bleaker than we imagine.

Yet, it is true that each person's individual power is close to nil. But, it is not zero. We are not powerless. If a connection to the Law is created for people in one's immediate environment, even if just one word such as *Myōhō*, or "Buddhahood"; or one phrase such as "all life is equal" is uttered amid the confusion and darkness of the time, it will have tremendous meaning. This world, this solar system, the whole universe is connected. If we can just say one word to people around us. Whether they take faith or not is their choice. But that effort which is a very small power, will eventually become the impetus for the best power for change. This is how I feel. This is what I believe.

On World Peace

There is phrase in Buddhism called *Kosen Rufu*. The meaning of this phrase given in the Lotus Sutra is to "spread the Law of NamuMyōhōRengeKyō in the world." The *kanji* characters for *Kosen Rufu* (広宣流布) mean to roll out over a broad area like a big cloth unfolding and flowing in the world. This is expressing how the Law of NamuMyōhōRengeKyō is delivered. It is flowing as if it is one big piece of cloth. But when I explain it in this way, people may misunderstand it to mean that the Law of NamuMyōhōRengeKyō will just spread, and the people of the world will take faith and correctly understand the teaching. But it is impossible for the whole world to take faith in the Law of NamuMyōhōRengeKyō .

In this world, for hundreds and thousands of years, a deluded way of thinking has evolved and become part of the culture, and misguided faiths. And the structures of the faiths have become the cultural heritage in countries throughout the world. There are some countries that are governed by religious belief. Their societies are built on laws based in their religion. Those laws have endured for centuries and millennia. It is impossible to destroy those societies and their laws, and force their people to believe in the Law of NamuMyōhōRengeKyō. If you force people to believe, it's no different than a tiger using violence to capture and kill its prey.

The group of people who hold the literal, utopian ideal of *Kosen Rufu*, that the whole world will take faith in the Law of NamuMyōhōRengeKyō, are not being realistic.

Another interpretation of *Kosen Rufu* is that even if there are people who, upon hearing it, oppose, question or are angered by the teachings, if any kind of connection to the Law of NamuMyōhōRengeKyō is made, then the Law of NamuMyōhōRengeKyō is being transmitted to the world. That connection is like a seed. When you plant the seed, that seed won't die. Though it may not bloom immediately, after a hundred years or so it's blossoms may appear. This is the correct mindset needed to deliver the message of the Law of NamuMyōhōRengeKyō to the world.

This faith of NamuMyōhōRengeKyō does not accept the denial or killing of people of different religions. To do so is wrong. Even though people do not believe in the Law of NamuMyōhōRengeKyō, each person, no matter what they believe, has Buddha-life inside them. There should not be any violence or discrimination carried out against people who have a different religion or a different belief. Nichiren

Daishonin's True Buddhism does not accept violence. It is important to believe with your pure mind.

The entire world will not follow these teachings or way of thinking. There are many people who will oppose it. Within each person's mind are certain beliefs. There is also doubt and conflicting ideas. Thus, the only way to connect the Law of NamuMyōhōRengeKyō to the world is through the method of what is called "reverse relationship" whereby people form a relationship with NamuMyōhōRengeKyō by opposing it.

I often use the phrase *issai shujyō byodo jōbutsu*, which means "all living things are equal and have Buddha-life within." Every life is equal. Every life has Buddha-life. This applies to all people in this world. And all life refers to not only human life, but all living things: all creatures as well as plant life. A bodhisattva not only strives for the salvation of herself or himself, but also endeavors, for the salvation of people everywhere, whether related or not, whether near or far, to spread the teaching of the Law that everyone has Buddha-life. That is the meaning of "all living things are equal and have Buddha-life within." This phrase, *issai shujyō byodo jōbutsu,* has the same meaning as *Kosen Rufu.*

Every religion, including Buddhist religions, believe that they are the best. They hold on to the notion that if the entire world believed in their religion, the whole world would be at peace. Or that the world will never be peaceful if people hold different beliefs. But, if the entire world started to believe in one religion, it is certain that some people would deviate from the religion, some would oppose it, some would be skeptical, and some complacent or negligent. And if that happens, perhaps the unfaithful will be punished, put death, or exiled. It is not possible that all believers of any religion will maintain pure and faithful minds, since within each human being is a mind that possesses good and evil. A religion that dominates the world will consist of some people whose "good mind" is dominant, and some people whose "bad mind" is dominant. Inevitably, contradictions and chaos would ensue within the religion, and in turn be reflected in the world. People would be forced to believe in the religion through threats and other means, leading to a dispirited, distrustful and oppressed way of thinking.

An example of this, though not a religion, is communism. Communism is a secular system created to achieve happiness for all. When you look at the former Soviet Union, China, North Korea and other communist countries people are discriminated against and killed for having their own opinion, or not strictly adhering to or believing in their systems of governing. These secular systems, established to make everybody happy, are controlled by a handful of elites who, in the end, have proven unable to make everybody happy.

It is therefore important that the individual decides on their own to take faith, or have the freedom to choose their religion without any coercion from others. This is the most important thing.

Towards the end of the Nichiren Shoshu liturgy is the phrase, *gyo do fu gyo do*. This phrase appears in chapter 16 of the Lotus Sutra, and means, *those who walk or walk not in the Way*. Since this is stated in the Lotus Sutra, it is an accepted fact that there will be people who will believe and people who will not believe.

Chapter 16 of the Lotus Sutra relays a story about a person who has three roles. First, he is a doctor, second, he is a father, and third he is a Buddha. As a father, he has many, many children. In his position as a doctor, he must take a trip and leave his children at home. As a father and a doctor, he warns his children that there is a very potent medication in their home that would be very harmful to them, so they must not under any circumstance touch it. As human nature is what it is, when told not to do something, human beings are tempted to do the opposite. So, the children found the medication and took it to see what would happen.

The medication was extremely toxic. The toxins spread throughout the children's bodies, and they became deathly ill, with many children passing out. When the father returned home and found all his children seriously ill, he was overcome with grief. But as doctor and Buddha he quickly began developing an antidote to cure his children. The medicine he prepared is NamuMyōhōRengeKyō.

The doctor/Buddha told the children they had to take the medicine of NamuMyōhōRengeKyō to cure them of the illness of having doubtful minds. By taking the medicine they could live correctly, and realize their eternal life. Although the poison had permeated the little bodies of the children, and some were near death, the father did not force the children to take the medication. He simply told them the medicine would cure them, save their lives, and lead them to the right way of living and a correct understanding life.

If the children don't believe what their father, who

is also the doctor and Buddha, says, and are not willing to take the medicine on their own inclination, the medicine will not be effective. Even though the children are dying, if the father forces them to take it, the medication will not work. Since everyone has their own mind, and mostly everyone believes they are right, there are some children who believe the father and take the medicine; and there are others who won't believe the father and will therefore not take the medicine.

This is exactly how it is in society. Some people might take the medication of NamuMyōhōRengeKyō, and some will not, even if their life or wellbeing were at stake. Thus in this world, some people will believe, and some people will not.

As far as I understand it, European history has dominated the history of mankind for a very long time. This history involves much violence. The majority of this violence is based on what is written in the Bible. And because the Bible is the standard, it is used to consider and determine the history of the past and present.

Mankind has been searching for freedom, equality and peace. But these are not written in the pages of the Bible. What can be discerned from the Bible is that human beings are nearest to God. It also indicates that superior life dominates inferior life, indicating that there is hierarchical classifications or ranking among life. This is an admission that there is no equality between lives. As seen throughout history, there has been Biblical justification for different forms or discrimination: the Nazis found that the Bible made the holocaust against Jewish people permissible; theologians found solace in the Bible to tolerate and even support slavery and discrimination against people based on skin color; and the Bible teaches female subservience and gender discrimination.

The Bible was not only the standard or foundation of society and world order in the past; it continues to be the back bone of society and world order today. In the past, priests were united with the crusaders, using the Bible and the name of "Freedom" to invade, conquer, pillage and rule "infidel" countries, and spreading discrimination and hatred in their wake. No freedom existed, which means no peace was achieved. The world which has the Bible as its center, or back bone, has only achieved discrimination, suffering and conflict.

Nichiren Daishonin taught that all lives are equal, every life supports each other, and that is what sustains the life of human beings. There is no rank among lives. This is why we must respect every single life. Of course, we eat other lives to survive. This could be considered the case of the stronger devouring the weak. But when considering that there is a life here that is sustaining my life, then we must express gratitude and respect for that life – be it animal or plant – that is nourishing each of us. By having this attitude and behaving in this way, absolute equality will be achieved. Freedom will be achieved.

Freedom comes when the Law of NamuMyōhōRengeKyō is placed in the center as the foundation and back bone. This is the freedom that liberates oneself. Without this freedom, peace will never be achieved. Peace can never be achieved by harming other lives with our pride. That is the basic teaching of Buddhism. Buddhism teaches us that we can't kill. Each person has to believe in the correct Law, not by force but on one's own volition. They have to have the correct way of life, live responsibly, and take responsibility for their own life. With this teaching of the Lotus Sutra, there will be comfort in the world. The teaching of the Lotus Sutra is the clue to achieving peace in the world.

What happens to our life if we don't practice true Buddhism?

Let's compare electricity to the Law of NamuMyōhōRengeKyō. For those who practice, the flow of the ultimate Law of life is always turned on. NamuMyōhōRengeKyō is there. It's always there, even in death. But if you don't know how to turn on the switch, you can't see. You are operating in the dark and you don't know which way to go. You will therefore be relegated to a lower state of existence in your next life. That's why it is so important for us to chant for those who have passed away — to open their lives, or to keep their lives open to the flow of this electricity — the flow of the Law.

VII

A Parable

Kankucho

High, high above miles and miles of untamed wilderness rises the impossible to reach Snow Mountains. Here bears roam freely, snagging fish from clear mountain streams. Snow leopards prey on deer. Snakes and vipers slither through trees and glide over the forest floor.

Without warning, geysers shoot sky-high streams of steamy mist, while unseen pools of quicksand lie in wait under fallen leaves to swallow up unsuspecting victims.

What cathedral could look more majestic, or look more dominant? What cathedral could be purer than these ever-white mountains, whose peaks are solid gold spires when reflecting the rising and setting sun? These mountains are bewitching, and awesome, beckoning all to come see.

Living atop a tree high above the dangers of these incomparable mountains is a bird named Kankucho. His name reflects his extraordinary beauty; a beauty which is as fleeting as the brief but vivid life of a butterfly.

When the sun goes down in the Snow Mountains, bitter cold sets in. The winds swirl the heavily falling snow, and lash and twist and eventually snap the brittle bows of trees. Kankucho sits at the end of a wisp of a branch, shivering and quaking as if he is permanently locked in the eight freezing hells. Ice forms on his back. And when he cries, frozen tears quickly pile up like stalactites down his face.

Kankucho's shrill and plaintive cries pierce the night. "My suffering is the deepest suffering of all," he laments. "My plight in this world is the most dreadful." His agony is intense. So overwhelmed by it is he that he promises himself, "Tomorrow, at day break, I will build a warm, comfortable nest. This I will do without fail. Never, ever will I freeze again!"

In the morning the sun rises. Its glow turns the icy mountain peaks to golden spires and caresses Kankucho. Gradually the bird thaws out and falls asleep. His sleep is deep and untroubled. As the day grows longer, Kankucho awakens content and warm, and trills a song of cheerfulness. He fluffs his downy feathers, and hops along his bow to locate a more comfortable place. Looking down below in the tangled jungle thicket, he searches for what will entertain him for the rest of day. Yonder a bear catches a fish. Nearby a leopard claws a rabbit. From high up on his perch, Kankucho witnesses other creatures playing games of life and death throughout the forest. Sitting at the top of the world on his wisp of a branch, Kankucho finds all is safe and secure, right and warm in the world. There is nothing that threatens or distresses him.

Day in and day out, this is what Kankucho does. He spends his days in comfort, and never gives a thought to building his nest. When evening descends on the Snow Mountains the bitter cold sets in, and Kankucho's shrill, woeful cries are heard piercing the white nights all the rest of his life.

Nichiren Daishonin used Kankucho as a metaphor to exemplify the life of human beings who are negligent and squander their lives pursuing meaningless things such as fame and fortune. We should use our lives instead to practice the Buddha's Law, seek the Buddha-nature within, and follow the principles of Buddhism to live a fulfilling and purposeful life. If we don't, we will repeat our sufferings again and again and again.

VIII

A Final Word

In This Time and Place:
A Buddhist Perspective

Chaos. That is the word that characterizes the state of the world today.

As citizens of this world, should we hate others because others look different from ourselves, hold different opinions, believe in different faiths, live in different countries, or come from different backgrounds and different circumstances? Aren't these differences the wonderful, natural tapestry of this diverse planet?

Namumyōhōrengekyō. That is the name of the Buddha-nature in every living thing. There is not a different Buddha-nature for me and another for you. Or a different one for able-bodied people and a different one for people of special needs. Not a different Buddha-nature for Buddhists, Christians, Moslems, Jews, Hindu, etc. Nor a different one for Central Americans, North Americans, Africans, Asians, Europeans, etc. and a different one for me or you. There's not a different one for plants and animals, water and air; nor a different Buddha-nature for the sun, the stars, or the entire universe. There is only one Buddha-nature— Namumyōhōrengekyō. What that means is we are all related.

Because everyone has Buddha-nature, and therefore all have the same potential to become Buddha, when you kill someone, you are killing the Buddha. When you disparage someone, you are disparaging the Buddha. When you have contempt for someone, you are holding contempt for the Buddha.

Namumyōhōrengekyō is a Buddhist Law. It is the Mystic Law of Cause and Effect. In addition to having this Buddha-nature, all life is equal and eternal. This is the teaching of Buddhism. It doesn't matter if you believe or not, it is just THE FACT of life. No one is above this Law; no one is exempt from this Law's workings. Our lives are determined by causes – thoughts, words and deeds – we make. This reservoir of causes is what is known as *karma*. On a daily basis, we continuously create good and bad *karma* for ourselves. The Buddha said, "If you want to understand the causes that existed in the past, look at the results as they are manifested in the present. And if you want to understand what results will be manifested in the future, look at the causes that exist in the present."[44] This means, it is possible that in the next life, any one of us could

---

[44] "The Opening of the Eyes," Part 2, *The Major Writings of Nichiren Daishonin*, (Nichiren Shoshu International Center, Tokyo, 1981), Vol. Two, p. 197

have the same experience as migrants fleeing desperate conditions, whether it's due to climate change, or violence, in Central America, the Middle East, Africa or elsewhere.

". . .If the minds of the people are impure," the Buddha wrote, "their land is also impure, but if their minds are pure, so is their land. There are not two lands, pure and impure in themselves. The difference lies solely in the good or evil of our minds."[45]

Buddhism views all life as basically good, because all life possesses Buddha-nature. But also contained within all life are the worlds of Hell, Greed, Animality and Anger. As human beings, we have a choice between expressing our Buddha mind and heart, or expressing our lower natures. At present, the baser, destructive natures in humankind are increasing in dominance, causing us to lose our pure minds and pure land.

It should be mandatory for world leaders to spend time in the International Space Station. If they looked at planet earth from that vantage point they would not see any borders. Instead, wouldn't they be awed by all this life

---

[45] "On Attaining Buddhahood," *The Major Writings of Nichiren Daishonin,* (Nichiren Shoshu International Center, Tokyo, 1986), Vol. One p.4,

sharing this one planet in an uninhabited solar system suspended in infinite space? Thereby, wouldn't they come to realize that we, in this time and place, are all related, and must care for and take care of this planet and each other?

Nonetheless, it is up to each one of us to seriously consider our actions, our words, and our thoughts because they are permanently recorded as our *karma*. Our individual *karma* and our collective *karma* not only affect ourselves, our communities, our country and our people, but also determine the viability of our planet.

Peach Pair

SOURCES

Dictionary of Buddhist Terms and Concepts, Nichiren Shoshu International Center, Tokyo, 1983

Discussions with Reverend Raidō Hirota 1999-2023

https://www.earth.com/earthpedia-articles/how-does-a-lotus-flower-grow/

Kirimura, Yasuji, *The Life of Nichiren Daishonin*, Nichiren Shoshu International Center, Tokyo, 1980

The Lotus Sutra, translated by Senchu Murano, Nichiren Shu, Tokyo, 1974

The Major Writings of Nichiren Daishonin, Volumes 1-7, Nichiren Shoshu International Center, Tokyo, 1979-1994

The Middle Way, Udumbara Foundation, Westport, CT., 1995-2022

Ohyama, Kendō, *Nichiren Daishonin and His Advent*, an essay, 1980

The Threefold Lotus Sutra, translated by Bunnō Katō, et al., Weatherhill / Kosei, New York, Tokyo, 1975

www.udumbarafoundation.org

ABOUT THE AUTHORS

REVEREND RAIDŌ HIROTA is a Nichiren Shoshu Shoshinkai Shukyō Hōjin[46] priest. He is chief priest of Sanbō-in, a temple located in Fukuyama, Japan. His religious studies began at the age of twelve at Nichiren Shoshu Head Temple Taisekiji in Fujinomiya, Japan. Since his ordination and commencement of his ministry in 1981, he has devoted himself to practicing, studying and teaching Nichiren Daishonin's True Teachings to anyone who wishes to hear.

PEACH PAIR is an American artist and a long-time parishioner of Sanbō-in temple, with 50 years of practice and study of Nichiren Daishonin's True Buddhism. She is the founder of Udumbara Foundation, and resides in Connecticut.

UDUMBARA FOUNDATION, founded in 1995, is an American 501(3)(c) foundation affiliated with Sanbō-in Temple. Its mission is to translate, and make available the True

---

[46] Nichiren Shoshu Shoshinkai Shukyō Hōjin – an independent, incorporated nonprofit organization of ordained Nichiren Shoshu priests, dedicated to protecting and teaching the True Teachings of Nichiren Daishonin.

Teachings of Nichiren Daishonin as taught by Reverend Raidō Hirota.

Cherry Blossom

Nichiren Daishonin died on the 13th day of the 10 month in 1282, which would have been late autumn on the lunar calendar. On that day, cherry blossoms bloomed throughout Japan. Thus, in Nichiren Shoshu Buddhism, the cherry blossom signifies eternal life.

Made in United States
Troutdale, OR
08/28/2024

22387335R00084